MJ Sinkey 2019

ON WRITING POETRY

For Poets Made as Well as Born

Al Rocheleau

Shantih Press
Orlando

Published in the United States by Shantih Press, Orlando, FL.

Library of Congress Catalog Card No.: 2010912343

ISBN-10: 0615396437
ISBN-13: 978-0-615-39643-9

Cover Painting: Kreidefelsen auf Rügen (Chalk Cliffs on Rügen)
by Caspar David Friedrich, 1818 (PD).

TABLE OF CONTENTS

for John Pietruszka

AN INTRODUCTION

Hello. Always nice to have an audience; perhaps I can help.

The chapters of this little manual, with the exception of a few added recently and specifically for the book, were written as separate articles over a period of several years, beginning in 1997. Many have appeared on multiple sites across the internet, and have been quoted, copied and relocated with relish, which was the intent all along.

This material has been utilized by high schools, colleges, and writing circles in the U.S., Canada, the U.K., and Europe; of course, I've been glad to see it so widely circulated. I've even found articles translated into French and Polish (I think it was Polish), so if you've tripped over any of this before, here's a chance to have all the pieces, spiffed up, updated and sewn together in a sequence that I hope you can use. As for this book's *actual* use to you, write and let me know. If I can be of further service at that time, I will.

Most of these pieces exist because it was simply *practical* to write them. In my work as editor / mentor at various workshops sponsored by magazines, professional writer's sites, and America Online, it had occurred to me that new and even working poets lacked the resources or instructions that could assist them BEFORE their work stalled, and AS they were writing.

In explaining to a new poet why something wasn't working for them or their readers, I found myself having to resort to the detour of actual instruction to fulfill a requested commentary or critique. In short, I wanted these hard-working people, regardless of their intent or style, to achieve a favorable outcome, not only for the poem at hand, but also, more important, for themselves as they continued in their craft.

This manual is not meant as an authoritative, academic text. Parts of it have been used that way by some here and there; that was not, and is not intended. There are, frankly, many more-detailed books available on the writing of poetry. Many are great, and I mention some of them here, while others are dry and dreadful. So it goes, and as with this casual fling at making good poets before you, *caveat emptor.*

Note that wherever possible, I have not changed the informal nature of the writing from the original, dashed-off nuggets meant to help a particular poet with a particular problem. Now, I do wax philosophic, even *rhapsodic,* on occasion; indulge me. But you'll see the text brims with familial "we's," with sprays of italics, bolds, and caps, and with by-the-way asides that engage conversation. In sum, these "briefs" are *supposed* to be light, friendly, and one-on-one. Hopefully, with recent edits and many additions, I have maintained those flavors, and you won't be intimidated or confused by anything here.

The book's layout may tell you: use this as a *course.* You could do it I suppose, but my *purpose* was simply to create a good *resource* from which you might take what you need and leave the rest. It's what I did in learning this craft, and it worked out.

Now, the title of the collection was intended to be *On Writing Poetry.* After all, it wasn't about dishing up good spaghetti sauce, or fixing a Volkswagen. My editor, however, prevailed on me to adorn the name a bit; so I borrowed, dropping a stitch or two, from old Ben Jonson's line, "For a good poet's made, as well as born." I think that's true.

While Keats, Rimbaud, and Merrill may have been "hatched" as great poets, most acquire their craft as they go. In doing so, they learn the existing rules of the road and, once knowing them, set out to *artfully* break them. They create great poetry stamped with their own brand, yet reflect both their contemporaries and forebears by elaborating on or outrightly changing styles, and even starting new traditions upon which other changes could be likely effected. In doing this, each poet advances the poetic art itself, the humanities in general, and in their own way, the society in which we toil.

Herein lay some of that "toil" part. And since toil, especially for the inexperienced, is made easier with a yardstick and decent tools of the trade, here's this manual. Use all of it, part of it, or consider you have a better idea than what you just read, and do that. But at least have a frame of reference, and like the poets who are around you and have come before you, a desire to communicate, to BE communicated to, and to help others along the way, as you are helped. It's what poets do. Even when such people are not writing, not publishing, they yet support the art of poetry, its existence, its perfection. And it is for him or her, the new or working poet, that this manual was written.

WHAT POETRY IS

There isn't really a single, satisfactory answer for this, since there is nothing more subjective than poetic thought. It is not just a form, it is a state of mind, a way of reaching something beyond the commonplace in the search for essential beauty, essential meaning. Was there more "poetry" in the music of Mozart than of Salieri? Certainly. More in mind and brushwork of Velazquez, than in all his era's imitators? Yes, fine. More in Fitzgerald than in Mickey Spillane? Surely the critics would say so. More in Bob Dylan than in the current en-vogue singer-songwriter? Yes for me, but most teens (and record-sellers) of the day might not accept that premise. Actually there's poetry, as a general import, in all of the examples, greater and supposedly lesser. And a lot has to do with just what aspects of art you've been exposed to, and how much of it, as to what you think of all that.

What about taking written poetry down to a **definition.** Can we? I'm not going to bother to go to *Webster's* for this, and maybe you have another definition, but here goes:

"An intuitive or organized writing which reaches a basic truth, or an essence of what object, idea, scene, or emotion it describes, both in the images it evokes, and in sound of its reading, whether aloud or off the printed page, and is effective both in immediate utterance of its lines and rests, and as an entire construction, separate from other writing to which it may or may not be considered attached."

Wow— pretty long definition.

Now, that idea of poetry can include a Shakespeare soliloquy, a psalm from the Bible, a paragraph of Lincoln or Martin Luther King, a Bob Dylan song; a chapter of Fitzgerald, Wolfe, or Kerouac, or even a semi-planned, off-color anecdote by comedian Lenny Bruce. Of course, the self-containment of such work assures that a few pretty, or pithy, yet otherwise *random* lines inside (unless cut away as its own sort of epigram, or philosophical saying) won't cross a dull, serrated edge of prose-style rhetoric to become *poetry*— an art that *sharpens* rhetoric's best devices (metaphor, simile, alliteration, etc.). Visceral in feeling and implicit in intellect, poetry can whet our senses with an impact as immediate as painting, sculpture, music, or dance.

So describing what literally constitutes written poetry is a tough assignment. William Carlos Williams's famous poem about a red wheelbarrow may not sound like poetry when you hear it, but when you look at it on the page, your doubts could erase. The poet has taken the commonplace and made it uncommon, isolating the wheelbarrow, the rain, and the white chickens, and bathing these images in a radiant aura of space. He grasps these objects, still or alive, alone or together, and makes them important, essential.

Fixed forms including sonnets, regular meter such as iambic pentameter or tetrameter, or rhyme schemes can tip you off that what you will be reading is "poetry." But those elements are literary *exercises* following rules that may or may not BECOME poetry, based on the skill of the writer, his or her knowledge of the poet's tools, and just what that writer has to say about something. That's why there's so much BAD material out there that looks like poetry, but *ain't.*

And, there's the difference: Polly-in-middle-school, and W. B. Yeats. Of course, with lots of work in those fixed forms, Polly might be the next W. B. Yeats. But even if she *isn't*, she can at least be Polly, reaching people who need and want to be reached with her craft and creativity as a working poet.

At the same time, what about *free verse?* Good and bad, it seems to be everywhere you look. Well, you learn— hopefully early— that just throwing words and phrases on paper haphazardly, or taking prose such as *"My cat died today. I am really sad..."* and breaking the grave saga over seven or eight lines (Williams's style, but not Williams's content!) doesn't wash— not at all. Just as Picasso knew how to paint "straight," T. S. Eliot, renowned for his many free-verse masterpieces, could write marvelously in fixed forms whenever he cared to. Craft (knowledge of metaphor, sound, and rhythm, among other devices) still rules the day, and really GOOD free verse, without the crutch of adherence to elaborate form, may be the toughest poetry to write. Yet on occasion, when a poet's labors in fact transmute his vision, the work becomes something stupendous, and enduring.

Often, in trying to explain what *is* poetry, you wind up explaining what *isn't*. But in the end, and this is a much shorter, if tougher, reasoning than we used before— if you have the INTENT TO MOVE A READER, SOMETHING ORIGINAL TO SAY, THE CRAFT TO SAY IT IN A PARED-DOWN, ESSENTIAL WAY, AND A READER TO SAY IN RETURN, "HEY THAT MOVED ME"— you probably have POETRY.

And with a little editing, you might even have GOOD POETRY.

IT'S POETRY— IT'S NOT PROSE

Most people who start writing poetry have at least some background in the making of prose. Whether penned by an award-winning novelist, or a teenage diarist, creating prose of any kind is natural to us. But it's interesting that both people above stand to fall flat on their faces when writing a poem. Granted, some novelists such as D. H. Lawrence and John Updike have also written great poetry. These artists, however, knew that the two disciplines have as many differences as similarities, and are, in essence, two different crafts. And a craft (or sullen art, to complete the Dylan Thomas phrase) takes work to master.

A major distinction between prose and poetry is that prose is directed right to the consciousness of the reader. While lines of prose can be very beautiful (witness Thomas Wolfe or F. Scott Fitzgerald) the basic role of prose is to inform, whether we are talking *The Great Gatsby* or "Dear Abby." Poetry, on the other hand, can exist on many levels, and mean many things, or in any specific way, nothing. In actuality, prose more often TELLS about things themselves rather than *showing* ideas, emotions, etc., through separate small details. (An exception is offered for some prose, including very good fiction, where the writer *will* do a lot of showing. In that way, fiction *can* be indeed similar to poetry.) But apprentices of *poetry* writing are told "show, don't tell" over and over again. It's a tee shirt-sized motto that finds itself among the cardinal rules of poetic art; would-be poets forget it at their peril.

Poetry is the essential written form, and is probably closer to music or painting than it is to all except the most "poetic" of prose. American poet Archibald MacLeish said that a poem should not MEAN, but BE. An oversimplification perhaps, but a good one.

As poetry, words are mosaic pieces measured and fitted, playing by themselves and with other words. They may not "mean" in any direct, intended sense; rather, they collect, *recollect,* in pools of significance at once universal *and* individual, fired off in kaleidoscopic display at the consciousness of each reader. The reader's experience then turns the words into effects as singular as was their writer's original cause.

In a poem, one is *always* examining how **sound** and **rhythm** are used, whether said aloud or "heard" in the mind. This isn't *sometimes* as in prose. Poets adhere to a simple law: EACH WORD IS IMPORTANT. They polish poems over and over, getting each word just right. Extras are avoided— "connecting" words are thrown out unless absolutely necessary. In short— EVERYTHING in a poem matters. Each word, every clash or confluence of words, paints a canvas into images (and sounds) to be interpreted, or just appreciated. Get the idea that words carry a value, separately and together, not in numbers, but in *effect.*

When people start writing poetry, they tend to write PROSE— only in "poetic" form. (Marcel Duchamp once turned a lonely urinal he called "Fountain" into "the next big thing in art." He was, of course, in on his own joke. New poets are decidedly *not* in on *theirs.*) Good poets soon learn that a fancy block of text only *looks* like a poem; poetic content and style evolve from it. Bad poets, oblivious, continue writing prose.

So, don't just *remanufacture* prose lines. If you can write your statement out in paragraph form, and it says exactly the same thing, *it's not poetry.* And don't drop off a message matter-of-factly, as if you were delivering a laundry list or a summons. Such blandness of phrase communicates something-or-other, but only at face value.

Example:

> I loved you so much
> and you left me crying
> how could you do it
> after that night in the park
> when I gave you what you wanted.

(Sounds like a suicide note. Perfectly functional as one— but it's NOT poetry.)

How about:

> These tears say nothing
> but reflect
> the winter's lamplight at this bench
> where I search
> for the me I gave you.

The latter statement reveals the same sentiments, without hitting the reader over the head with them. Let the reader search his OWN experience to connect with you— don't give them yours. They don't need that; they don't want that. They need a new look at THEIRS. By telling less and *implying* more, you reach core emotions, core associations, core intellect, each prize available in each reader. In short, you *connect.* Remember— don't tell it—SHOW it.

Do that, and you've signed the lease for a fine career in poetry. Now, we lend you the tools and perspective needed to fulfill the terms.

POETRY— OUT LOUD OR ON PAPER?

Poetry acts on us through sound— pitch, volume, consonance, assonance, rhyme and cadence, as well as through the process of visual translation from print on page to a mind image. In doing the last, one takes into account the overall sculpt of the poem as it lay on the page, the ease of assimilating the words, and the words themselves as they fall into a kind of "silent" aural experience— building meaning or at least, "impression," word by word, stanza by stanza.

The actual sonics are much the same, but more immediate— the sound hits us, the dynamics of loud and soft, stop and start are less delayed, more forced onto the reader as if he or she were given a good shake. Hopefully a poem is crafted well enough to shake a reader silently, too, despite any inherent delay. (To check, try reading it aloud, then silently.)

Most poets, indeed, most poetry, does benefit from being **read aloud**. Whenever possible, I read poetry, from beginners that I'm editing, to master poets in the *Norton Anthology* or in their own collections, aloud. Usually, you will pick up a good deal of intended inflection and hidden dynamics that way, and it will probably lead to a deeper understanding of the poems, of the craft employed, and of the writers themselves. The poet's personality can really jump out of a piece when you read it aloud, "playing" at both punctuation and line breaks as the composer directs— not just stopping at the end of each line!

One of the best experiences I ever had with poetry was while I was on a trip, alone in a hotel room, reading aloud fifty or sixty pages of Shelley. (Poetry is, if nothing else, a noble time-killer.) Shelley's poems, like those of Dylan Thomas, Gerard Manley Hopkins, or James Merrill, have their own sonic plan; often sound is more important than literal meaning— and reading such poems aloud can be a revelation.

(One may note that experiments with *sound alone*— minus or severely minimizing syntax and meaning, have been going on for more than a century in the work of such poets as Lewis Carroll, F. T. Marinetti, Andrej Belyj, Kurt Schwitters, and more recently, Bob Cobbing and Allen Ginsberg. Whether the experiments "go too far" is a question of how long the tape measure is. From epic incantation of ancient bards, to ecstatic "tongues" of shamans— **sound** is a basic of all poetry of all times, and every poem we read uses it to greater or lesser effect.)

At the same time, there are those who employ their words and lines in such a calculated, "page reliant" manner that they are, as elected, best read silently. For me, the list includes William Carlos Williams, E. E. Cummings (although he is actually a very good reader), some of the Beat poets, the "concrete" poets (whose poems are based on space, shape, or graphics) and Wallace Stevens, a modern Romantic whose precise, intricate work is richly philosophical and at times, difficult— almost as if it's challenging you to dwell on each phrase as you go along. Not surprisingly, Williams and Stevens are two of the *worst* readers of their own work (my opinion only) that you will find among the major poets.

In any case, reading aloud was how poetry started (remember Homer), and it can yield great benefits to HEAR our poetry just as we hear the music of the world. When you're writing, read your work aloud as you edit, and when you read others, try doing the same. It is enjoyable, and it will help your work along, too.

ACTION VERBS: YOUR POEM'S ENGINE

New poets tend to write a line at a time, as if the line, or well-turned phrase was everything. Actually, it isn't. Your poem must flow, and move, line by line, stanza by stanza. To do this, you use action verbs, preferably in the straight or "simple" form, tied to a subject. "I RUN," "the wind SKATES," "they ESCAPE," "we CRY." These verbs all denote ACTION. The subject / action verb combination, in the simple form (whether present or past), followed by and effecting itself upon an *object*, is at the core of most good poems, just as it is in prose.

Now, if you use a participle verb form, e.g., "I *am* run-*ning*," "the wind *is* skat-*ing*," "they *are* escap-*ing*," "we *are* cry-*ing*"— the helping verb TO BE softens and dilutes these statements, so they end up not as strong. You can use such forms at times, but be aware of that softening. Also, know that **modifiers,** including *phrases* or *clauses,* must tie clearly to a **subject.** In particular, watch for **participles** and *their* phrases. Don't "dangle" them far from home, or use them alone, pretending they are *action verbs*. True, an **elliptical clause** can *imply* its subject or verb without including them, but untied fragments can't assume that weight. Such "disconnects" stall poems— avoid them.

Remember: **ACTION VERBS** ARE THE ENGINE THAT MAKE YOUR POEMS MOVE FORWARD AND GAIN STRENGTH, NOT HOVER AND DIE. Put verbs to work— and don't write in fragments. Poets whom you *think* wrote in bits and pieces (Williams, Cummings, the later Plath, Bukowski) were using *elliptical constructions*— within the poems were continuous lines, strings on which subjects, verbs, and objects, used overtly or very clearly *implied,* carried the pieces to their ultimate ends. Whether fixed form or free verse, a poem MUST move.

You get a lot of mileage out of the **sentence form** in a poem. In the first example below, you see *fragments,* phrases not combined— lots of crooked stops that imply little and lead nowhere. It begins with a weak linking verb ("am") attached to a lonely adjective— no *action verb* in sight. Nothing happens. Who did what? In what way? Why? Then notice the "flowing" just hanging there among bland, mildly accusing bits in a passage unclear, uninspired, awaiting cue cards.

> I am sad. Tears flowing, *not good*
> Sadder than I've ever been.
> Because of you.

don't use present participles

The second example (below) is essentially ONE sentence. Stanzas are often one continuous sentence, propelled from an isolated image or premise, to a definite conclusion. And the way you make your lines *move,* just as you do in any effective sentence, is by using action verbs. Make your lines DO something, not just BE something. (Expanding on MacLeish's idea.)

> I drive this deaf
> nail into the wall;
> penetrate sheet-rock
>
> the chalk of you.

*(Ouch! The second one MOVED, didn't it. While the language might have seemed, on its face, less "direct" in arriving at surface meaning, the **effect** of the lines was VERY direct, and **deeper** than the obvious.)*

REPEAT— DON'T USE A STAND-ALONE PARTICIPLE OR A PARTICIPIAL PHRASE IN PLACE OF A SUBJECT AND SIMPLE ACTION VERB. In our first example: *Tears flowing.* (Not good).

A fast way to spot an amateur poet is the abuse of "-ING" (present participle) or "-ED" (past participle) words left out alone. Tears flowing (can tears do anything but fall or flow!). Snowflakes dancing. Bodies flying. *Yesterday?* Girl abandoned. Snow expected. Cannons aimed. Don't use such phrases as detached fragments. They don't advance a poem as direct *action verbs* do, obeying *subjects* and affecting *objects.*

Before:

> Missing you.
> The night is so long. Tears flowing.

How about:

> You miss these tears.
> But the night counts them,
> a metronome, a measure
> of me.

Now, you CAN use participles as helpers in a longer poetic sentence. For instance:

SEA GRAPES (EXCERPT)

The *surf* would pull them in
with its lithe, foam grips
if it could, **feeding the plump
berries** to the ghosts of sharks
who no longer require blood.

Above, "feeding the plump berries" is a **(present) participial phrase;**
it ties back to the statement's subject ("surf"). And another example,
slightly different:

AMONG THE GAS GIANTS (EXCERPT)

I'd read somewhere
that the seventh *planet*
spins backwards,
tilted on its side,
frozen deep away
from a pinprick sun

Here, **(past) participial phrases** ("tilted on its side" and "frozen deep
away"), are tied to a *subordinate clause*, and its subject ("planet").
You'll use such phrases all the time, lining your poems with gorgeous
upholstery and detail. Apply participles *that way.* Attach them to their
subject; never "hang" them out alone, pretending they are action verbs.
As in an **action** film, the **verbs** you have mastered await the command
of that *locomotive* that is your poem, in the scene that is *your vision.*

GETTING ON WITH THINGS: LIMITING ADJECTIVES, ADVERBS, ETC.

Prose has time to make breakfast, clear gutters, clean the attic. Poetry does not. Since every word in a poem must be *essential,* acquire in the lines a monk's discipline— avoid what doesn't need to be there. This includes words that modify nouns and verbs— the adjective and the adverb. While these descriptors can sometimes color a noun, or better define a verb, you'll find as you continue building your craft as a poet that you tend to use the adjective and especially the adverb much less.

What will take their place are vibrant, exact, original **nouns** (both as subject and object) and much stronger **action verbs**, working in tandem with **subordinate clauses** that will include *even more* of the same. There will be a lot of action, and less dwelling on single nouns and verbs laden with clusters of adjectives or adverbs. In other words, you'll *get on with things— get on* with the poem. It's interesting that as you learn to fold in the powerful devices of simile and metaphor, adjectives and adverbs become the egg nog and ribbon candy you only pull out at the holidays.

In attempts at formal, metered verse, a new poet often resorts to injecting adjectives, adverbs, or other words as filler to "feed the meter"— which means adding an extra word to a line that requires a set number of syllables or beats. This is probably the WORST reason to employ an adjective or adverb. Rather than do this, just extend that poetic sentence (noun + action verb + object + subordinate clause) onto the next line— the carry-over called **enjambment.** (More on this later as the process earns a chapter.) Within a line or two, the statement will tend to finish itself off without any artificial forcing at the end of a line, and you'll be fine again— with no trail of useless, annoying filler words.

Adjectives and adverbs describe well when an extra line isn't there to use, and a feature *must* be known just then. (If you *have* extra lines at your disposal, describe with noun-or-verb phrases, or with, as we cover later, *metaphors and similes.* But when adjectives or adverbs appear as mere interlopers, they *clutter.* Remember: "flow" in a poem is FAR more important than decoration, and any *unnecessary* words you include will fight against the premise. On that, let's trim a little.

> Dark and restless, sleepless nights
> turn slowly to the respite of the dawn.

How about:

> Wide-eye nights plead
> the dawn's respite.

The new version: *one line of pentameter OR two lines of free verse.* Here, I'd consider changing "respite," accent on the first syllable, to "reprieve," accent on the second, so long as meaning isn't affected, as the line's rhythm is now different. Anyway, we've cut back adjectives a bit and chucked the adverb that was tied to a so-so metaphor, one we reduced to a possessive phrase. When you try on adjectives, think of them as jewels— tempting to wear, sure, but you risk that gaudy look! And strong action verbs can afford to lose the adverb that tags along as a stage direction. Use adverbs when you *must,* or not at all.

Beyond adjectives and adverbs, constant use of "of the" (as part of an *adjective phrase* in the first example) presents its own problem. While the "of the" linkage can add a dram of dignity to a particular line, it also REALLY slows a line down— so unless that is your intent, consider changing the "of the" phrase to a *possessive noun phrase* ("dawn's respite," rather than "respite of the dawn") in order to reduce the line.

Finally, put in the articles "a," "an," and "the" only when you need them— but don't be afraid to use them at any point. The intransigent "no-articles" school produces as artificial-sounding and wrongheaded a line as does the affected and overly ornate "faux-romantic" school. Just COMMUNICATE, straight-on, with as much impact as possible, making EVERY word count. All those interesting word-types, those "parts of speech" we mentioned, have their place. Just make sure they occupy *that* place, and no other.

ABSTRACT CONCEPT WORDS—
AVOIDING THE NO-SHOW

There's a tendency for new poets to use concept words that identify an idea or emotion, but do nothing to SHOW what those words mean.

use a lot

"Love," "life," "death," "hate," "truth," "fear," "spirit," "soul," "beauty," "grief." There are a host of others— the common symbolic, "non-object" nouns that stand for very broad concepts. These are usually words to *avoid* in a poem. You must show these concepts; don't just say them. By themselves, these words mean nothing to the reader.

In fact, if you use one of those words, you can almost bet you just weakened your poem. It might take one fine phrase to evoke "hate," or a stanza to really explore it, or an entire poem to revel in it. Don't just say "hate." Using the nebulous word "soul" in a poem is usually akin to holding up an identification sign for a stranger at an airport. You know—"HERE I AM!!" Only, your reader shouldn't *be* a stranger. Let them get to know **you** (avoiding your "soul" or, except as the center of something, your "heart"), and through you, to know some part of themselves, by showing them some bit of the tangible, *real* stuff of life. Be inventive with sound, with images, with scene-setting, with the building momentum of lines and stanzas. As soon as you resort to a rote concept word— you have begun to tell, not *show*— and your poem will die as in the following example:

> Love dwells within your soul,
> you see the beauty of life
> through him.

Instead, how about:

> There are those who can neither see
> the filament that glows and drives your chosen saint,
> however slowly, to his source.
>
> You are not one of those, of course.

The latter example has something to do with love, devotion, duality, immortality perhaps— without using those concept words to say any of that. Invent; illustrate. Spend some time working your lines in an original way, and leave the dumbly symbolic concept words on the slates of those lonely chauffeurs at the airport.

THE "POX" OF CLICHÉS: PREVENTION AND CURE

[handwritten annotation: transcend the easy, common, routine.]

The sequence of chapters may be cause for apology, as there's a "poet's priority" we should have noted at the beginning. The fact that we didn't might qualify this instructor for more than a parking ticket, but something slightly less permanent than the guillotine. In any case, I throw myself on the mercy of the tribunal, and we discuss the subject now. (OK, what am I *talking about,* and *why* am I talking like *this?*)

If there is one thing the new poet must learn, and every working poet works hard to remember, it is this adage: STAMP OUT CLICHÉS.

In reality, I opened this piece with a cliché. How many times have you heard "he got away with no more than a *parking ticket.*" While I used a variation on that overused saying, I still used it— parking ticket. Perhaps I could have said I deserved more than a "wink and a 'case dismissed'" instead of that same old parking ticket. See? And I sure could have done better than "throwing myself on (your) mercy," too.

Poems by new poets, quite understandably, or by ignorant, inveterate lifetime amateurs, not-so-understandably, are often rife with clichés. You'll also cross paths with dumb-looking, archaic words such as *'tis* and *o'er,* or those tell-all concept words, e.g., "love, "soul," "spirit," used *o'er* and *o'er* again (all of these examples are inherent clichés)— but with this vital subject of *clichés in poetry,* we should go much deeper. Rejecting informal turns-of-phrase that populate speech and prose, the goal of any poem as an essence of thought or emotion, is to transcend the easy, the common, the routine. For us, clichés must be avoided like typhus (not the plague), and quarantined by this advice:

REGARD ANY WORD OR PHRASE YOU RECALL HEARING USED A CERTAIN WAY MORE THAN ONE TIME, INCLUDING ANY COMMON IDIOMATIC PHRASE (unless you can use it with a clever irony) AS A CLICHÉ. Watch for these items! Don't fall into their trap. (Oops, I just used a cliché there.) Don't mistake doorknobs for diamonds. (Well, maybe not *that* phrase— is it mine? You know, I don't even recall.) Establish your own way of gift-wrapping an idea, delighting, as I'm currently doing, in *metaphor* and *simile*. (We'll talk more of those benefactors soon enough.) **Please, let others copy you!**

And then, on occasion, as with Eliot's cruel April and Shakespeare's mortal coil (among a half-dozen phrases in just *one* soliloquy), write something that sticks so hard in the psyche, no one could even TRY to copy it! Either way, those lines will arise from, or at least, alloyed and invigorated, will pass *through* that rather special poet that is *you*.

STOP poetry that looks like this:

MILK OF MAGNESIA OF HUMAN KINDNESS

You have soothed the savage beast within,
and I have walked a razor's edge to reach you
yet now, just now, it finally dawned on me
the lessons that a laxative can teach you.

You get it. ("Get it" is an overused idiomatic phrase.) Come up with a new "savage beast," or "razor's edge." Perhaps a "Savage Beast II: Moloch in a Leisure Suit," with Pauly Shore (oops, let's replace him with Adam Sandler), Charo (for the "senior" set), and other walking (or macarena-dancing) clichés. You see, the stars of today generally become, quickly, just like phrases, the clichés of tomorrow. It may seem hard to be that inventive at first, but you CAN do it; something will "dawn on you," and you'll "teach yourself a lesson." No kidding. "No kidding," in itself an overused colloquial expression."In itself," another overused, awkward phrase. Choose your language carefully. Better yet, invent it. Yes, you. YOU invent the next cliché, one that, at least for a time, you can use with impunity. Be original, an actual trend-setter, or *something like it.* Know that *all* the great poets (and most every lesser good one), have celebrated their very own uniqueness of language, their own private brand of "cool." Oh yes— yes we know, *cool* is—

MORE ON MATTERS QUAINT, COSMETIC

Digging further into what words, phrases, etc., to avoid... (and geez, drop those dumb dots in your work, will you!)... it's worth underscoring the *quaint, cosmetic things* in your poetry, and ridding yourself of them. As we'll explain, those dots, the **ellipsis**, make your lines trail into nothing, destroying the poem's momentum. It is *not* cute, this device. Despite its oft-employment in prose (including in this book), constant use of the ellipsis *in poems* will likely be, all "pregnant pauses" aside, as successful as mating two mules.

On **centering lines:** in past centuries, many poems were centered on the page. One can still expect to see such layouts in greeting cards, scrolls, and plaques. Frankly, I like the visuals of centering, but I don't normally use it my work, nor do most contemporary poets. With the exception of some free verse, Western poets work from the left margin, as prose writers do. This doesn't mean *you* can't center the lines of a poem, or parts of one, but constant use of such rich framing borders on the precious or at least, the antiquated.

About **old words**: throw out words that don't fit your time— those *archaic* words, *old usages*, and *contractions* that don't fall and fit on the contemporary reader's ear. As we mentioned, the "'tis" and "o'er" belong in another century. Such contracting within or between words (called *elision*), either to show your "poetic" side, or just, *God 'elp ya,* to shorten a line to meet a metrical requirement, is actionable in any court of taste and talent. It's important that you employ not only the right words, but also words in the *right definition* for the time at hand. The word "for," for instance, sounds contrived today when, as a conjunction, it replaces "because." Slowly, definitions *become* archaic.

You know better for you are smart— and yet you fain take part?

Consider changing the "for" there, and please cancel the "fain," which had begun its death hacks before the Rossetti siblings took up their journals. In addition to *whole* words becoming archaic (shopworn, ill-fitting)— particular *usages* of a word do the same. A good working rule: if it sounds "old-fashioned"— punch it out, kick it to the street.

Those of you who are stuck in the Romantic or Elizabethan periods, and use flowery-sounding poetry, as Robin Williams so deftly put it, "to woo women," try taking the subway out of Suckling and Shelley once in a while and translate their beauty into your own time. There is great substance in Shelley too, by the way, just as there is in Shakespeare. But you must detach from their language, and savor the import on a new tongue. Sound or image may join two eras— but not *speech.*

It's only good sense. Nowhere in Shelley or Shakespeare will you find idioms and descriptive words penned in Chaucer's Middle English, any more than in Chaucer's *Canterbury Tales*, will you find the Old English of *Beowulf.* Appreciate the beauty and profundity of a poetic period for what it is— don't copy its veneer, because, believe this, you won't do it justice, any more than the language style of Chaucer or Shelley would do justice to Dylan Thomas or Auden. Remember, your time is just as beautiful in its way, and most certainly just as profound.

And besides— I'm almost sure of this— you can woo women easier when they know what you're talking about.

ON METER

Some heavy stuff here. Don't worry, we'll cover the material from various angles throughout the book, lightening the load as we go.

Writing good poetry is not easy. Harder still is the writing of poems **in meter;** yet, virtually every new poet attempts it. That makes for two things: a flustered writer who can only approximate what he means, and an uncomfortable reader who begs relief. Caught in the straight-jacket of iambic pentameter or tetrameter— singsong lines sounding like da DUH, da DUH, da DUH, da DUH, da DUH (*pentameter,* or drop one da DUH, for tetrameter), patterns you were forced to absorb from some *Awfully Famous Poems* anthology— you sought to imitate. Boy, did you (someone turn off the metronome!). And if you *then* add to this equation a search for *end-rhymes*— there you have it: a mess.

The concept of the **iamb,** in which a weak syllable precedes a strong, stressed or accented syllable, is a basic of human speech, at least in English. So is the use of lines or phrases, separated by a breath, that carry four or five such stressed syllables, in which meanings of words are emphasized. **Pentameter,** in which five major stresses (sometimes called *beats,* since you can beat them out with your hand) are present, is considered our natural means of poetic expression. A majority of Shakespeare's lines and perhaps 70% of all literary poetry in English are written in pentameter. Open any anthology of poetry— you'll find pentameter (usually *iambic* pentameter, five stresses to a line), or its shorter, minority cousin *tetrameter* (four stresses to a line). As for the the actual rhythm of these lines, the "iamb" part of the phrase "iambic pentameter," as well as all of the iamb's relatives that can otherwise define the meter (trochees, dactyls, etc.)— more on them later.

*(By the way, when analyzing the line construction, or **PROSODY** of metrical poetry, you will hear the word **FOOT** used regularly. The term applies to a stressed or accented syllable PLUS the weak, unaccented connecting syllables sounded before or after it, taken up as a **measured unit**, and making up one word OR several words within a line. As such, you can measure that line according to its number of **feet**. Poems may rise unconsciously, and yet, can be **very** consciously plotted in number and type of feet for each written line. A pentameter line has FIVE feet, tetrameter FOUR, trimeter THREE, etc.)*

Actually, it's harder for most poets to write good tetrameter than it is pentameter, simply because they have less room to say what they want to say before the line ends, and less space to vary the line so that it doesn't sound metronomic, predictable, and *boring*. In truth, this is when people decide they don't like poetry— when it doesn't reflect how we talk. A silly dilemma— since, if you plot out the stresses in people's speech, they do talk in four-stress or five-stress phrases most of the time, and, focusing further, in actual weak / strong *iambs* a lot of the time. Just not *all the time*.

While you may be able to take a poem and count out the stresses within individual feet of iambic pentameter or tetrameter, NOT EVERY FOOT needs to be iambic. There are many ways to shape lines of poetry. Take that last sentence. It could be "scanned," in the measuring process called **scansion**, this way (STRESSES are capitalized):

there are MA	ny WAYS	to SHAPE	LINES of	PO et ry
(anapest)	(iamb)	(iamb)	(trochee)	(dactyl)

Stripping the words away, it *sounds* like this:

```
—  —   /   —   /   —   /     /  —    /  —  —
da  da  DUH * da DUH * da  DUH * DUH da * DUH da  da
```

Weak syllable is a "—"**(dash)** or **"da;"** a **strong (stressed) syllable** is a **" / "(slash)** or **"DUH."** Separating each **foot** is an **"*" (asterisk).**

Now, the line we chose is a *prose* line, not intended for a poem, not planned as meter, and not crafted in any way. Even so, could that line be made an acceptable part of a poem based on iambic pentameter? Examined for its effect on the ear, it doesn't fall, at least as-is, under the design of iambic pentameter *(it's not da DUH da DUH da DUH da DUH da DUH)*— see a difference in the stresses? Our prose line, reflecting spoken English, had a few weak syllables thrown in, and had two stresses side by side. Given that, would the line still work?

One should keep in mind there are variations in the way readers pick up a line's rhythm— but with a few clippings, that random example could pass as a line of *mostly* iambic pentameter. Just know it wasn't a *poetic line* when we began; it wasn't planned that way. We tried to *scan* it as one. To pull that off, we would have to transform the line under the existing set of rules, so that prose becomes verse. You see, lines are elastic—easy to work into systems of meter, since the dominant stresses, the *strong syllables,* are natural to speech in English.

That elasticity factor is vital. Why? Because we are not robots, we vary things for effect— it's the way we talk. Sometimes it's smooth and predictable, sometimes it isn't. So don't make your sonnets, your blank verse, or *anything* based on five stresses, or even four stresses, sound so "da DUH" predictable. WRITE LIKE YOU TALK. The content of most great poems in English is not pristine iambic pentameter, line by line. As time went by, from say, the time of Alexander Pope to the Romantics, the purely metronomic iambic content of poems went (and this is admittedly a wild estimate) from about 95% to 75%, then to the current modern approach, which averages maybe 65%. (This penchant varies of course, from poet to poet.) One can suppose that beyond relaxation of academic rules, people talk differently in different periods, and so they write differently, too. Remember this: YOU CAN COUNT OUT AND CONSTRUCT ANY TYPE OF METER WITHOUT IT *SOUNDING* EXACTLY THAT WAY WHEN READ.

Now, if we tried to *force-scan* that previous line, making the pattern ALL weak / strong *iambs*— the staple of iambic pentameter— our example would not endure even if you dropped normal speech inflections, and just read it aloud or to yourself as stiff, repeated, weak / strong syllables. It just would *not* work. Look:

there ARE   ma NY   ways TO   shape LINES   of PO   et RY

Scanned that way, attempting to force rigid adherence to the concept of weak / strong *iambs* in every line, you would mentally have turned this line into *hexameter*, or *six*-footed. AND it would have become unintelligible in terms of actual *utterance*, actual speech. Sometimes poets will stretch a bit to fit an iambic pentameter or tetrameter pattern. A line may technically scan as iambic pentameter, but we would never adhere to that plan when the poem is actually read, either silently or aloud. In this way the construction of metered verse *becomes* that elastic exercise, elastic *in degree,* based on the daring of its creator. You *can* bend, you *can* stretch. Adhere too rigidly— you'll stultify the language. Stretch too far, of course, and you can audibly break your form, if an overall form was planned.

For these ears, and hopefully for yours, the *first* scan of our line worked better, even if it wasn't a great line. Why? Because it is the most *natural*. Now, could you have written that line some other way, used other words, and come out with five *natural-sounding*, even iambs? Yes, you could, but then again, you always risk that metronomic-sounding *monotone* we mentioned at the beginning of the chapter. Many lines will work fine all-iambic— but not ALL the lines.

Our options in writing these poetic lines reflect the pervasive meter format called **accentual-syllabic meter.** For more than six hundred years, back to Chaucer in the 14th century, Western poetry has mostly followed this theory-as-practice. Within the meter and all the verse it produces, both *vocal stresses* and *feet* are considered, with the latter measured as various combined units of weak and strong syllables.

There are also other meter traditions, largely gone unused, that are based *entirely* on vocal stresses, with no attention to syllable counts or line length **(accentual meter)**, OR, conversely, on strict counts of an *unalterable* number of syllables in each line **(syllabic meter).** Beyond the specialist or new proponent of these disciplines, the majority of poets and academics hold to that ultimately ubiquitous arc-welding of the two poles— the **accentual-syllabic.** Some poets, including me and others known to me, not to mention those who are suitably famous (W. H. Auden, for instance), lean back, and perhaps *forward* in time, to a style that may not abandon foot construction, but accepts the natural dominance of vocal stresses— of writing the way we talk, since that is also, intrinsically, the way we tend to listen.

Consider it— writing like you talk. Relax your phrasing; be natural. You can still have the meter you planned on— five stresses (or four for tetrameter), but the delivery will be based on where the stresses actually exist in speech. Remember *elasticity.* Read the lines ALOUD, beat the stresses out with your hand— you'll find them, and generally, you'll get consensus on where they are.

You'll find that when you talk as well as write, you create plenty of iambs. But since you also vary your speech with various inflections, any of those may alter, often favorably, various "feet" within lines of your poems. Don't just think **iambs**— weak / strong, weak / strong. Count actual stressed-and-unstressed syllable combinations of ANY kind as they lay within a line. In other words— write as you *say* it.

Stand up. Don't be the serf whipped into fitting sets of stresses into truncated statements that must end with every line *because of meter.* Write your phrase or your sentence *naturally.* If the statement falls to the next line, then *to another—* that's just fine. Don't add little words (DO, VERY, SO, etc.) to stretch a line out, or alternately, ruin a thought by subtracting a stress. If it doesn't come to five stresses, but you like what you said— take a pause there, a comma, a dash, a period— whatever works, and consider starting your next statement or phrase *before the end of THAT line,* and then continue it into the next one— the process of *enjambment.* This beginning and ending of statements on different lines creates a "ribbon-effect" that speeds up a poem, and keeps your meter sounding natural rather than forced.

One trick that works well for some poets (I use it often) is to draft the original poem as free verse, then pour it into a mold of either tetrameter or pentameter, nipping and tucking lines here and there, enjambing some phrases to the next line— just seeing what works. Sometimes it will end up in one form, sometimes the other, frequently neither— then it will either stay in free verse or you can *invent* some kind of form. However, try letting the form come to you— don't bow in unswerving servitude to its commands, or like many newcomers to poetry, you'll seem to deserve the bad poems that you write.

It's true that the use of **form,** as well as various concepts or constructs we call *meter,* can shore up the underpinnings of a poem. Whether we are conscious of it or not, as a group we gravitate to order, and also to cadences. This "marching" advances— with the arts as its catalyst, and *poetry* as its voice— a culture that we as individuals go on to invent.

Just make sure that in following the various, often *prevaricated* rules of meter, you don't lose that voice, *your* voice, that which you really wanted to say, and in the way you wanted to say it. Because, mark this— if you cede such invention to a slavish obedience, you've just wasted your time, and worse, you have likely wasted the reader's.

PO et ry is TOO WON der ful and PAIN STAK ing
a PROcess to WASTE in the FUM bles of FIXED ME ter.

Da DUH da DUH da DUH da DUH my FOOT.

Loosen it up, will ya? And have fun.

METAPHOR AND SIMILE: WYETH, CHAPLIN, BLOOD, AND SOMETHING LIKE AIR

The use of **metaphor and simile** may be that area that most separates struggling new poets from the published, or at least, "working" ones. An ability to illumine (or somehow *enhance*) the commonplace is the poet's greatest gift, and there are no more viable tools for the job than the metaphor and its cousin, the simile.

Rather than just making a matter-of-fact statement, the metaphor or the simile gives us ways to make a statement even "more direct than direct," if that's possible— in short, to make it something transcendent. The items arrest and stir in their frame like wind through the lace curtain of an Andrew Wyeth painting, creating a gulf of possibilities that no longer remain as just window, curtain, and air.

This effect is created not merely by describing with decoration, such as using adjectives and adverbs or, in Wyeth's case, applying strokes of paint, but also by juxtaposing objects and action in colorful, distinct arrays that may remind the person of *another* thing or time, another idea or emotion. The comparing of "like wind through a lace curtain" is a simile. The idea of vastness transfers to "gulf of possibilities" as a metaphor. ("More direct than direct?" That's an *exaggeration*— or near-relative of our featured pair, called ***hyperbole***.) As a reader, what may any of these phrases "say" or "do" to you? A complete answer rests with whoever *you* are. That's the purpose of metaphor, simile, and other rhetorical devices— to expand our *own* outlook, to open windows of our *own* experience, and in so doing, to gain for each of us a greater understanding of the *depth* of a love, the *degree* of a hate, the *purity* of a soul. Now, what exactly ARE simile and metaphor?

A **simile** is a *comparison* of two things, using a phrase that begins with "like" or "as."

A **metaphor** is an actual *replacement or transformation* of one thing for or to another, not just a comparing— an actual REPLACING in the context of a statement or image. Get that difference, or *distance.*

> Desire like a blast-furnace
> consumes me.

(That's a simile [like a blast furnace], a comparison of two things using "like" or "as.")

> Lust falls down two flights of stairs.

*(That's a **personification,** a type of **metaphor** where a thing becomes a person [Lust falls down...]. **ANY** metaphor creates an **implicit** bond, usually one that was not considered until it was specifically offered by the writer and accepted by the reader. The object, concept or person **transforms** into something or someone else— the abstraction that is "lust" can't fall down stairs— but its imagined "body" can, and did.)*

Now, let's take it further. You need to watch out that you don't MIX your metaphors, juggling too many different TYPES of images in the same work.

> Lust falls down two flights of stairs.
> I say hello to her;
> shivering like a featherless penguin
> I move to speak again.

Line 3 is a different image totally *out of left field* (itself a bad metaphor!)— it doesn't work well with what came before it. Once you've laid down a metaphor or simile, be consistent with it. You are not just writing cute, isolated lines— you're writing a POEM, a work of art that builds upon itself as it goes along.

How about:

> Lust falls down two flights of stairs;
> dusting off, the courtier's hello
> comes out Chaplin—
> not only the stance, but the sound.

Here, we reinforced *one* metaphor idea (slapstick, *silent* comedy), and kept the personification of lust— ***without*** naked penguins. Remember that each metaphor must *align* with each other one, since a reader has to track the transformations. Otherwise, the phrase loses any sense save that of a forced cleverness that doesn't survive past its own line.

We could also have used "it comes out LIKE Chaplin" (a simile, the *external comparison)*, but there was no reason for that extra distance. Sometimes, just the hint or flavor of sameness is in order, and similes do their work well then. But if you want do "go for the throat"— use metaphors. Just make sure they're GOOD metaphors. Select with care, and don't combine unrelated metaphors and / or similes. A random act of neglect or hubris here will pull the reader into a revolving door and tumble them back onto the street, Chaplin-style.

Understand that metaphors could be used anywhere in a poem, and should be matched with others like them. Also, the *entire poem* can be a kind of grand metaphor, an ongoing transfer strategy that goes right to the poem's core, and as a force, *evolves* with it. This painstakingly figured structure is called an *extended metaphor.* The poet draws out various aspects of that general metaphor idea throughout the poem, and may alter meaning in subtle or profound ways. So in this case, a metaphor isn't a small part of a poem— the metaphor IS the poem.

Point of fact— I once extended that "slapstick" metaphor in another piece called "Fall Downstairs with Me." In it, I selected images that would forward this clumsy, stumbling motif in what was, in fact, a love poem. There, a metaphor changed not one thing, but everything.

Now, you may find yourself using more *similes* at first— that's fine. Metaphors, *like young bulls,* (a simile) come of age with advancing bravery— just don't be reckless with your use of them. *Recklessness often tries to pass for bravery* (metaphor of personification— concept as person), *but comes out merely foolish* (another one). Work your metaphors very carefully, and only keep the ones that really work. If you start a poem with one type of metaphor— stick with that type, but also, *never beat one symbol relentlessly to death.* (Metaphor again!) Once learned— and the learning comes with the gradual comfort of employing them— these *deliverers* will not desert you, or you, them.

In sum, good similes and metaphors can so improve and invigorate your poems you almost won't believe it. Your reader, meanwhile, will delight in your invention. Fluid, indelible, they *pair in poetry's blood* (metaphor); they *refresh like night air* (simile). **OK, *one more:*** in a lit, reflected world, their mirrors turn and tilt; at your service, they shine.

THE BEAUTY AND CURSE OF RHYME

New poets usually start out writing in **rhyme.** An appetite for pairing similar / identical vowel sounds at or near the ends of lines, is nurtured by our exposure as children to the playful sounds of nursery rhymes. We advance to simple poems learned in the elementary grades ("The Night Before Christmas"), and court finally the lovely rhyme schemes of all that daunting Shakespeare and Tennyson assigned to us in high school. Unaware of our own options as fledgling poets, we regret the loss of never-found readers as we flail and flounder in rhymed forms.

Rhyme is one of the poet's most powerful sonic tools, and like any such sharp, vibrating appliance, you can slice off your fingers or bore out an eye. My advice to most new poets: *leave rhyme alone*— at first, *completely* alone. The reason is that rhyme can become both a pretty intoxicant and an abusive wire coat hanger which together dominate what they purport to help, in the best (or worst) "Mommie Dearest" sort of way. (For reference, see the Joan Crawford bio.) The new poet is too easily remanded a slave to rhyme, fishing for rhymes, tortured by rhymes, and altering thought in order to feed the all-holy *rhyme.*

Once a poet has learned the craft of poetic statement, and developed his voice in the academies of free verse and of metered, unrhymed blank verse, rhyme allows a palette of colors and sheens that takes one's poetry to another place. The instrument of rhyme, fused onto line-ends *(external)*, or set inside lines *(internal)*, chimes along with other sonic bells in fixed and free forms alike, electing readers to its trance. But first, *the apprenticeship*— it arrives in steps. Armed with some command of voice, then form, *then* sound, a poet can proceed to write without fear in rhymed meter, like Shelley, Keats, Coleridge—

any of the greats who intimidated you in years past. At that point, and only at that point, the discipline of rhyming may actually help you to define yourself as a poet. For some, that time may come much later— each to his own progress. With that preamble, can I repeat the advice?

New poet, or poet new to rhyme— use rhyme **sparingly** at first. Ease into its world. Outside of fixed-form poems you are *ready* to write, don't resort to rhyme as a regular practice, or especially, as a crutch. Try occasional end-rhymes, internal rhyme (better), or use none at all.

Before:

> I see you now, and all the time
> beyond my feeling, in my mind
> I see you though you're far way
> today, tomorrow, every day.   (a greeting card reject)

Instead, how about:

> I've stretched to you, arm's length
> on a frozen day, the shadow-dance
> plays havoc in drifts;
> then the sun
> goes away.

(Here the rhyme is a little less predictable, hidden, where it can be used for best effect. Rely on the image, not the rhyme. Never force your lines to accommodate a rhyme. NEVER.)

If you *are* a new poet, try busting right into free verse. Just write what you REALLY want to say, unworried about paying a "rhyme debt" at the end of a line, and break those lines where the mood, the "feel" strikes you. Get your voice, and eventually, that marvelous voice will ring not only with truth, but also with the timbrels of selective rhyme, tamed and mastered by a poet who refused to be encumbered early on by an all-too-seductive *device*.

When you're ready, there's more to be said about rhyme and other sonic wonders, and it will follow. But remember, new poet, Ben Jonson's admonition:

> It's a Rhyming Age, and Verses swarm at every Stall...

Jonson wrote the line, for the sake of too many bad poets, about four centuries ago. Somehow, even with the marked reduction in stables today, and need for shovels, the quote still applies.

Don't let it apply to you.

SO, YOU'RE GOING TO RHYME ANYWAY, ARE YOU?

All right. We advised caution for new poets on the use (and misuse) of rhyme, yet we know that some of you *are* ready to use the device well, and others are going to pretend they are anyway. So what the heck, let's talk a bit more about rhyme.

"MASCULINE," OR SINGLE-SYLLABLE RHYMES (RAIN / SPAIN) ARE MORE POWERFUL THAN "FEMININE," OR MULTI-SYLLABLE RHYMES (SPINNING / WINNING). It has to do with the direct nature of a single, forced syllable on the ear. As soon as you go to two-syllable rhymes, a softening occurs. "Sweet" poems tend to have a lot of multi-syllabic end-rhymes. (Look at Shakespeare, or at "Cavalier poet" John Suckling.) *Comedic poems* depend on these rhymes, as does today's rap poetry, which revels in them. But use the rhymes carefully. Understand the effects, because they can be like pink packets of saccharine in your coffee. Unless the intent is to be sweet, or funny, use more single-syllable rhymes.

> There once was Drover from Dover
> whose sheep disappeared in the clover.

(Feminine rhyme awaiting punch line, perfect for bars.)

But how about these lines:

> For through it all like horror runs
> The red resentment of the guns.

Robert Service— the lines are from "Foreword" in his wartime collection, *Rhymes of a Red Cross Man*. In poems like this, unless irony is intended, you are likely to see dark, one-syllable rhymes. Now, what if *runs* and *guns* are changed to *running* and *gunning*? See the softening? From John Dryden's *heroic couplets* of the 17th century, on to this day, we enjoy the *impact* of the masculine rhyme's one syllable.

OFF-RHYMES (BELT / DELVE, FROND / LAND) ARE LESS OBVIOUS THAN EXACT RHYMES. Off-rhymes (also known as *slant-rhymes*) may *begin by matching* vowel or consonant sounds, but *end differently.* OR, they can start differently, but the *end-sounds match.* Below, consider *mixing* exact and off-rhymes in your lines.

Here you stay	Exact rhymes only.
in my way	
I can't think	
sleep a wink	
you're a bum	
I'm so dumb.	

Instead, how about:

Here you stay	A mix of exact and off-rhymes:
in wake	stay, belay, wake (exact and off-rhyme)
and bobbing blue —	you, blue, truth, anew (exact and off-rhyme)
belay the truth!	
(your signal lost)	lost, Cross (off-rhyme)
my tiller's fixed anew	
upon on the Southern Cross.	

Now, you can get real technical talking about rhyme— of families immediate or removed, pedigreed or "illegitimate." But the major dynamic plays out in the interrelationship of the exact and off-rhyme. As you progress, you'll learn that those two, one scrubbed, one not, often work well together.

Such things as **identicals** (lay, Mandalay), and subtle, visual-only **eye rhymes** (least, breast) are considered worthy by some. (I use both on occasion, and poets of the past used them all the time, especially the latter.) Yet, deployment of those designs (and of *off-rhymes,* even) are considered bad form by others. Hmmm. I suppose that's why there are Catholics and Protestants, with or without capital letters. Let's just say, *use what works for your own ear.* If it does, it will probably work for the reader, too. **Note:** READING ALOUD helps you **hear** the sound effects you create. Do this— read aloud.

Know, too, that you can control the effect of rhymes by the **distance** you place between a word and its rhyming mate. Too many rhymes too close together can ruin a poem rather than perfume it. (It's like pouring Chanel No. 5 or Halston on your head, rather than dabbing it on your neck). The further away a rhyme actually hits— not only on the same line but also separated by many previous lines— will soften the effect accordingly. This calculated spacing of rhymes works especially well in internal rhyme schemes— rhymes that do not necessarily come at the ends of lines (the "wake" and "belay" of our previous example). Fixed forms will tell you where and how to rhyme.

So (big pause), we're trusting you to use the device of rhyme wisely, or not at all, right?... OK? (Yes, now we can sleep at night...) Enjoy.

THE SOUND OF THINGS

You've heard the saying "words are a poet's paint," and that's true. But there are different types of paint, different textures and an array of colors and combinations of colors to be used. In this case, as in music, poetry's close cousin, we are talking of "sound-colors." This all starts not with the syntax (how language is put together) or semantics (what things mean), but with basic *phonology*— how things SOUND. (And linguists, bear with me as I purposely over-simplify classifications.)

If you're writing a pretty poem, a sentimental poem, a love poem— you will probably choose to write with a lot of soft-sounding conso-nants; these are **f, l, m, n, r, s, v, w, x, y** and **z.** When you do see hard consonants, they are usually tempered by adjoining soft consonants such as **gr, pl,** or **ch.**

You could use many of the vowels **i, e, a**— the "highest sounding" vowels of the quintet (in descending order), and you would likely use them in their pure, or *long* form, just as if you were reciting the letters **a** (face), **e** (seen), and **i** (line).

You may also find yourself using many *multi-syllable* words, and if you're rhyming, multi-syllable (or feminine) rhymes, since this softens the sound of lines.

When you're writing a darker poem, you may use more percussive consonants— **b, c, d, g, j, k, p, q,** and **t.**

You also have the "low sounding" vowels **o** and **u.** Augmenting these shades are the dissonant notes of the poet's musical scale, what I call "discolored," or *short* forms of vowels **a** (bat), **e** (bed), **i** (bit), **o** (bog), and **u** (bug). The impact is revealed in a survey of offensive or explicit (dirty) words. Most of these words contain: one syllable; percussive consonants; low-sounding vowels or, if vowels are higher **(i, e, a)**, they share those drab, off-color forms **(-ick, -iss -it, -itch, -etch, -ex, -ang, -ock, -ong, -uck, -ut,** etc.). Fascinating, if you think about it.

It's important to remember that *one-syllable* words of whatever kind reach the reader quicker than multi-syllable ones, and the percussive, short word does count in terms of immediate impact. *Anglo-German* words tend to be shorter and on the whole, more percussive, hence more immediate. *Latinate* (and some Greek-derived) words tend to be multi-syllable and on the whole, softer sounding and far less immediate in impact. Do you want the reader to think or feel? Do you want the poem to move fast, or slow down? You control this by your use of Anglo-German vocabulary (*feel* and *fast*), or Latinate vocabulary (*think* and *slow*). All things equal— modern poets have gone a bit more for the former, while traditional poets, rather more for the latter.

Anglo-German	Latin-Greek
tough	formidable
kiss	embrace
molt	exfoliate
pluck	courage
food	sustenance
thick	viscous
rude	impertinent
dung *(among others)*	excrement
dirty, crude	explicit, offensive, obscene

There is no right or wrong in choosing which words you want, except that it's good to know something of your *intent* (the sound that will hit the page, and your reader's ear at any point) as you write. In truth any poem that contains ALL Anglo-German, single-syllable words, hard consonants, and low-sounding or altered vowels may just be *too* heavy and dark— oppressive.

Likewise, a poem with ALL Latinate multi-syllable words, with high-sounding vowels and all soft consonants might kill you with its over-bearing sweetness.

They key is to *mix* them for the effect in a particular line, stanza, or through the whole poem. For an example, compare Dylan Thomas's "Fern Hill," to his "Refusal to Mourn the Death by Fire, of a Child in London"— the first is all **s's, l's,** pure **i's** and **e's.** The second is far more mixed, with altered "high" vowels and some low **u's** and **o's** thrown in, as well as a higher concentration of single-syllable, Anglo-German words. Was this all conscious? Not really.

This use of phonology is partly *unconscious*— a writer tends to do this naturally, depending on subject matter and emotions involved. But a *conscious* knowledge that there exists a full palette of available sound, on the order of a painter's color wheel, makes our poet more of a sound-master— a musician of sorts and in the process, more of a poet, too.

ALLITERATION, ETC.— PLAYING WITH THE SOUND

Alliteration in fixed or free forms, is a sound device which adds a dappled, trance-like sonority to a poem. Part of the "rhyme family," it is the repetition of *consonant* sounds at the *beginnings* of two or more words ("love's lead laurel"— all the **l's**), while what we *usually* call *rhyme* involves repetition of *vowel* sounds at or near the *ends* of two or more words. Alliteration appears like wildflowers, all over poems. You must know several near-relatives to alliteration and rhyme, too.

Consonance involves stringing **mid-word or ending** *consonant* **sounds** together among two or more words ("somnolent, beneath such ignorance" or "a tin of rain within the garden"— check the middle **n's** you find in that former example, and those ending **n's** in the latter.) **Assonance** involves stringing **beginning or mid-word** *vowel* **sounds** together among two or more words (like "adrift, ajar, asunder" or "vague, slate, unembracing eyes"— check the **a's** that begin words in the former, and the **a's** wrapped *within* words of the latter). As with any decoration, use of such ornaments is easily overdone. So...

USE THESE DEVICES, *ESPECIALLY* ALLITERATION, SPARINGLY. As we covered earlier with rhyme, too much sound-playing turns the cake into "all frosting." See below.

Before:

> Pompeii's frozen, frantic forms,
> fill and frame a thousand furrows,
> forgotten.

Instead, how about:

> Pompeii's frozen forms, a thousand
> cast for time
> out of one mind's many,
> framed in happenstance, harmed
> and harmless
>
> wait, as we for nothing
>
>   wait, and get it.

There, the **f's** are pruned and ***broken up,*** so the effect isn't relentless; I blended in, too, **3 h's,** *plus* some **m's** and **w's,** giving the reader other twists. You'll note one more device, a word repetition ("wait"), added not only for sound, but also for emphasis of that word's meaning in what would be a larger poem. (Eliot used such repetitions all the time.) Of course, you don't have to be so elaborate. Always, a *statement* that drives the work is more important than any tricks of the "artful" poet.

Also, if you can get used to stringing *consonants* elsewhere than the beginnings of words (as in the middle or end), using **consonance,** or perhaps clustering high or low vowels at the beginning or middle of words to create light or dark effects, using **assonance,** then you vary your sound arrays even more. Remember, adding space and distance between like sounds make the effects more subtle. As we have said about **rhyme,** be judicious in your use of *all* these devices— but enjoy making poems that reflect the beauty of the language.

CONTROLLING THE FLOW: LINE BREAKS, PUNCTUATION AND SPACE

Poets often have trouble with the overall construction of their poems, not knowing how to control a poem's speed, where to break lines, and where and how to end. Well, try thinking of a poem existing as a flow of water down a hill. Gravity is naturally pulling upon it. Undisturbed, neither channeled nor dammed up, it will flow speedily down to a level plane, its ultimate destination. So it is with poems.

With water, aqueducts can be erected to channel it, and dams to stop it altogether within a reservoir. Valves can be installed to limit the flow, or have it gush out in quantity as needed. With poems, and with words as water, you have structures— line length, meter, space / indents, punctuation, and line / stanza transition— that order and transform this otherwise natural flow, creating a variety of effects.

When a line is short it will tend to move the reader to the next line quickly.

Example:

> When a line
> is short
> it will tend
> to move the reader to
> the next
> line quickly.

New poets tend to write in longer lines. Often, that's a holdover from prose writing. Sometimes, lines have to be long to capture a whole thought that *needs* to fall on the eye all at once, but this is not usually the case. Of course, there are fixed forms— tetrameter, pentameter, and even hexameter, where lines of set stresses have been preordained. It's like putting your poetic voice on a hanger— the content is artificially held up by the form. This is a test for the writer, as every line must be filled with meaning and music to keep the reader's attention. When it's done right, great poetry results. This was the discipline of poetry pre-1855. (Essentially, pre-Walt Whitman's *Leaves of Grass.* Whitman, by the way, wrote in very long lines, almost prose passages; his poetry definitely ebbs and flows off every extended exhortation.)

After Whitman, formal verse remained dominant for fifty years— but now, poets could experiment with original subjects, and with different line lengths to alter a poem's flow. When doing the latter, the intrinsic feel of *meter* was not lost— it just tended to divide into more than one line on the page. (Note that Emily Dickinson innovated privately in this period, affecting later generations.) When we finally reach T. S. Eliot, William Carlos Williams, E. E. Cummings, and the Beats, short line free verse is common, interspersed with longer lines. Such poems flow quickly, unless of course, the poet wants to stop the flow.

To do so, to stop things, a longer line (or lines) will do the trick. But make sure the line "feels" as if it can't be broken. The thought and language must be strong, because the reader will focus on that.

Changing meter from a flowing one (like say, iambic pentameter) to a hard, stopping one, or one with hesitation, where you then run to catch up with the basic meter, will slow down the reader, as well as add interesting variations from time to time. Use of words and phrases that stop and start work in fixed forms as well as in free verse. We've said that a poem in very strict iambic pentameter (da DUH, da DUH, da DUH, da DUH, da DUH) can be monotonous unless you're displaying some artful invention within the lines, as Shakespeare, Pope, and Shelley did. Since we are not them, and since the rules have changed a bit, allowing a more natural (for us) use of language, we take advantage of that latitude. Of course, should you rely too much on changing the meter stress, you will make things overly choppy for the reader. The art of balance is something you learn as you go along. Remember, poetry is supposed to flow, unless at a particular point, you decide that it shouldn't.

LINE BREAKS— Five different people could break off a line to the next line five different ways. The key for you is to decide how fast you want the reader's eye to fall to that next line. If you carry thoughts over to the next line, using *enjambment,* it will definitely *speed* your poem's flow, as opposed to ending your statement predictably at the end of one line, then going into a new thought beginning with the next line. Enjambment is a great way to spice up and speed up fixed forms as well. A few of these enjambments, well-placed, can often improve a poem a great deal.

But in free verse, where to break the line? *You have a lot of choices.* First you want to keep track of the overall sculpt of your poem, how it appears on the page. The narrower the sculpt, the faster it flows. Regarding individual lines, try breaking at various points and see what speeds up or slows down the lines, according to your desire.

If you stop after a noun, the effect of the break may not be as quick as if you break after a verb. It would be quicker still if you break after an adjective, adverb, preposition, or conjunction since, in about that order, you are moving away from subjects and objects first, then actions, to descriptive, directing, or connecting words— in other words, you're moving further away from the way people put thoughts together. If you break after nouns, the reader can "rest" a moment— he or she gets an immediate image of something. But if you break after, say, a preposition, more information is needed to form an image (reader asks, "where is this taking me?"), so the eye darts quickly to the next line. You can also play nifty semantic games with line breaks, as in the following:

> Lust
> falls
> down three flights of stairs.

The word "falls" literally fell. Verbs that denote movement work well for this. (Note, too, how words *tumble* in line 3.)

Of course, you have to watch the meaning of your lines when you break, too. If the break clouds your meaning, do you want that break? Or do you want it *because* it clouds the meaning, perhaps in a way that could open up other interpretations. In any case, good line breaks come from a subjective process. Experiment. Just remember that different breaks support or inhibit speed, so choose according to your plan.

SPACE— has tremendous value. Poetry is at least half a visual exercise. Space will stop the reader's eye, whether using a small indent, or completely isolating a word or a line to the far right or wherever, or skipping lines (one or more) for new stanzas. The more space used, the more the stop.

PUNCTUATION— is the writer's "musical notation," used to slow or "rest" the flow of lines. The slow-downs are called *caesuras.* You can hesitate, "breathe," or stop at the end of a line, or in right the middle of one, by employing space or punctuation. It may be this capability that most separates the professional craftsman from the amateur; *how* you will do it depends on your style, and on choices for each poem. Just as Horowitz, the great Russian pianist, had 20 (or 30) dynamics of loud and soft, fast and slow in his keyboard work, so the poet learns to control the currents and contrasts of lines and stanzas. There is a parallel between music (especially for me, classical piano music) and poetry— arts comparable not only in creative intent, but also in composition and performance.

Types of Punctuation:
Period— stops a line. Not a jarring stop, and with no expectation thereafter. You just start up again.

Long dash or double-dash (NOT a hyphen)— Stops with a jar. There is expectation of what will immediately follow.

Comma— very small rest, and most common of our caesuras. Know that the *end of a line,* if part of a phrase or clause is *not* carried over, is a rest unto itself. If you add a comma, you are saying "on this particular line, stop just a bit longer"— one of the many "shades" of slowing— remember Horowitz.

Colon— a lesser cousin of the long dash or double-dash. Not as flamboyant, nor as foreboding a stop, nor as frequently used.

Semicolon— a useful stop, stronger than a comma. It ends a thought, or part of one, sometimes *inside,* and more often, *at the end of,* a line or stanza.

Exclamation point— a stop like a period, perhaps slightly more so, but calls a lot of attention to itself. Limit use.

Question mark— not so much a stop as a complete STALL. It is hard to use questions well in poems. It can be done, but more often than not, it will stop a poem dead. The reader is not reading so much for questions, as for illumination, for answers. Don't use a lot of questions (and question marks).

Ellipsis— the dot-dot-dots... be VERY careful how you use these. They will tend to hang up a poem, make it hover, kill a poem's momentum. I can count maybe five poems in thirty-five years where I've used an ellipsis. As a rule, substitute a long dash (or double-dash), semicolon, or period in place of these.

Know that you can substitute *units of space* for some of the punctuation marks, or add spacing in addition when you think it's necessary. You're the boss on this. Remember that too many stops can stall your poem. But also know that if you use no punctuation and no spacing, you are going to have one FAST poem, perhaps too fast to carry a lingering message. In time you will come to appreciate the "balancing act," and use these methods consistent with your strategy for the poem.

TRANSITIONS— Sometimes poets will write in fragmented or isolated thoughts, in lines that don't connect to the lines that follow. They will also write *stanzas* that fail to coordinate with *other stanzas.* Transition is vital; without it the reader waits for missing cues and *bogs* mentally mid-poem. Think in terms of **sentences.** *Subject* and *objects.* Use *action verbs,* and add *subordinate clauses* sometimes rather than ending each line or stanza as a completed statement. If you don't, your poem will slow down A LOT. Relate each stanza to the next. Consider connecting the stanzas by simply continuing the sentence. That will add speed and seamless flow to your work.

And how do you know your poem has ended? Well, have you said the *core* of what you wanted to say? If you have, you could find that if you follow the flow of the poem, it will *tell you* when it's over. When you feel it is, ensure that you have closed with a line, lines, or stanza which ties elements of your poem together, creating the knowing calm that comes with water that has flowed downhill, and despite the rocks and veering eddies along the way, has reached the plane of its destination. You know what they say: *water seeks its own level.* Don't stop working your poem until your music and message have reached their level, too.

ENJAMBMENT— DEBUNKING THE FLAT EARTH THEORY

Poets have a tendency to think in *lines*— but lines don't make poems. They just make lines— which is why *group-invented poetry,* each line floated in turn like a burnt offering, doesn't work very well. What is left is a collection of separate ideas— related maybe, or not so much, containing sounds and images however pretty, yet— *not* a poem.

When starting out, most poets (and far too many when continuing to write) commence a thought at the beginning of a line and stop it AUTOMATICALLY at the END of that line. The same goes on with EVERY line— they just STOP at the end. Now, if we all spoke in that clipped, monotonous manner (you know, like those detectives in the TV show *Dragnet*)— we'd drive each other crazy! Well, don't drive your reader there, or further, drive them away from appreciating your voice. Express that voice, make that complete statement of yours, and if it takes you into the next line— GREAT! This is not the Flat Earth Society, who believe that if you don't stop at the end of a line, you will fall into a fiery hell. Quite frankly, if you don't buy into such fear, you may occasionally approach the opposite destination, taking your reader along. All right— how do you cross this "point of no return?"

It's called **enjambment**— and it works in both fixed or free verse. (Are you aware that a healthy percentage of Shelley's lines, in some of his greatest poems, are enjambed, and it's done each time without compromising the fixed meter of either lines involved? It's really not hard.) You simply carry over phrases (thoughts or parts of thoughts) onto the next line. A thought's completion may not require the entire next line—instead, it could stop midstream with a period, a semicolon, a dash, or a space. Then? We start *a new thought,* which itself will end on the line OR, carry over, too. People arrange ideas in compact units; such units catch the eye. Should *every* phrase or clause stay entirely in its line, however, conditions get too *predictable.* If the reader expects that a statement will always finish itself off at the *end* of each line, they will also prepare to stop, slowing down your poem and retarding its overall effect. At various places, you might throw in a phrase that carries over to the next line *on purpose,* just for the ebb and flow of it all. Enjambment wakes the reader up and allows him to fall quickly to the next line. It keeps the reader interested and speeds the natural, vertical descent of the poem, like unfurling the foresail on an old caravel, or for us, pressing on the gas pedal of a car.

Consider "Träumerei." (Lines 3, 5, 6, 8, 11, 12, 14, 15, and 16 are enjambed.) This poem was cast in a kind of accentual meter, with focus on beats, not feet; it is a pentameter poem, but would not scan as customary *iambic* pentameter. The example shows that anybody can enjamb, even if you don't have Shelley handy. There are many enjambments here— often, one or two such allowances will do the trick— you don't need to overdo it.

TRÄUMEREI

I embrace the brick enclosure of my youth in tears,
memories pulled like light-shafts from an unfull quiver
impossible to fire at the heart of my yearning, but I
can remember, when gay macaroni painted gold
on a cardboard candle holder was like filigree
to the crown of Clytemnestra, when the Ten Family lent me
a sugar cup and I returned happily with the difference,

when sky was at the top of the page, when the house was a box
with a pointy roof, when I was not swallowed by blue
or confused by angles, when war was unequivocal—
the standing or knocked over plastic men, when the smell
of paste was sweeter than chrysanthemums adorning
any soldier's grave, sticking doilies onto hearts—
and when attraction to a girl was the crinkle
of her nose, the sweetness of her being, worn on the face
without affectation, and I fought to be at her place
on the dancing circle, to marry in the momentary,
holding hands for real, in the church of children.

Beyond controlling a poem's speed, enjambment guarantees your thoughts their full expression. Sometimes you have more to say than fits on one line. Dropping down grants full flower to your message, without compromising it or truncating it. *You keep your voice,* rather than surrendering to the blind dictatorship of the SINGLE LINE.

Flexibility is vital; *you* can decide whether or when to carry down part of a statement. The enjambment option may also liberate your poem's meter, since you will not need to "hedge-clip" in order to fit a planned stress count; even when you drop, the old line's rhythm stays intact. This method worked for Shelley, and it will work for you, whether it's applied to fixed meter or to free verse.

Most of the time, you won't end a line with an article or conjunction— it will usually be a stronger word, a verb or noun, or more occasionally an adjective, adverb, or preposition— but it still goes by "feel" and the poet's intent. Now, in "Träumerei" there is no enjambment in the last lines, as it was time to slow the poem down. (Remember, enjambment speeds things up— it's predictable line endings that "tap the brakes.")

So that's enjambment— good for explorers of oceans or open roads, for those who reject that shy-away from the end of each line, that safe, sorry Flat Earth Theory. You could say we are "lifting horizons," or "making worlds go round." But since I'm out of metaphors, you can simply catch a ride on this handy exercise, and see where it leads.

THE PERSON YOU USE

So many poets start out by writing what has come to be known as "confessional poetry." And some— Berryman, (Robert) Lowell, Plath, Sexton, and others continued on to greatness with it. Poets will focus on this genre through an urge to explore (for celebration or catharsis), their personal, emotional highs and lows— love, death, the various trials or triumphs of life. Because this drive involves a necessary, but narrow introspection, it's natural that much of its release is bonded to the first person— using the pronoun "I."

While many great poems have been written with "I," countless BAD poems also have. The reason is that "I" is *so* personal, the poet can often leave his or her readers behind. No matter how compelling the subject matter may be, the "I" denotes it happened (or is happening) to YOU— not necessarily to everybody else. For "I" poems to work— indeed for any confessional poem to work— you have to involve the reader, making personal affairs universal by focusing on fragments of an issue rather than the overall issue, parts of your story, rather than a whole story, and veil your events in the gauze of simile, metaphor, and other tools of the language. In other words, don't confess like they do on daytime talk shows or to the police. Confess, instead, with a breath that will change as it passes through the horn, to be heard by another set of ears in a different, then perhaps, universal way. And when you use the "I," try not to get too narrative with it— "I did this, I did that." Focus on the small things *surrounding* to tell your story, rather than what's "inside" of you. A good way to know if you've succeeded in that is to count in your draft how many times you wrote the words "I" and its possessive, "my." How many of them could you have avoided? Generally, the fewer that remain, the better.

One suggestion to avoid the pitfalls of me-me introspection is to use the pronoun "you" or "it" instead of "I." Remember, you can still "confess" from a distance— like leaving a gayly wrapped package on someone's doorstep, rather than just saying— HERE YOU GO!, and pushing yourself in their face. Using "it" will automatically create some distance, some breathing space.

Using "you" works well too, since "you," a bit more distant than "I," still lends itself to some very direct statements. It's just not used as often as the confessional "I." Some famous second-person examples are Sylvia Plath's "Daddy," and quite a few of Anne Sexton's poems, such as "All My Pretty Ones," and "Divorce (Thy Name is Woman)." (Actually, speaking to one's parents, spouse, or children is common-place in the "confessional" vein— although the content of the above poems is far from commonplace.) Since many new poets are drawn to introspective writing, and many will *stay* in that area, I recommend they read the poets mentioned to get a feel of that confessional side of life's report, when "the gloves are off," but when craft is surely *on.*

The pronoun "they" isn't used as much as "it," but "they" denotes the same fiber of distance. The final pronoun is one with which you must take care— yes, "WE." Since "we" can be as direct as "I," its singular twin, parallel warnings are in force. There is, however, an *additional* caveat— the assumption that the reader will automatically count him-self as part of the "we." Don't bet on it. Using "we" is chancy, because it is *so* easy to sound like you're preaching when you use that pronoun. Yes, we use "we" throughout this book; we're *poets* here, *colleagues.* When you're writing on the unresolved issues of *mankind,* however, that "we" might sound like: "Endowed of great self-pride, I deliver my pronouncement. You're in my thrall— listen intently; agree totally."

Occasionally, it works. T. S. Eliot soldiered unafraid with the first person plural in his riveting climax to "The Love Song of J. Alfred Prufrock" (1917):

> We have lingered in the chambers of the sea
> By sea-girls wreathed with seaweed red and brown
> Till human voices wake us, and we drown.

Eliot used this "we" again, also famously, in 1925, characterizing men as hollow, scarecrow-like, and goes on over several pages telling just how "we" are that way. He uses "we" with profit years later in his *Four Quartets*. In all these instances, Eliot employs that point of view with such scope of intellect and craft that you'll buy it. At the same time, he supports these observations with an array of evidence that shines a stark, objective clarity, accompanied with music, or its opposite— a cold silence. Eliot's grounding, not only in master poetry, but also in religion and philosophy, made for a pretty knowledgeable guy. *OK, back to you and me.*

When you say—

> We are put on this earth to love and not kill.
> We must leave the world better than when we arrived.

— the urge is to say back, "oh yeah— that's so easily said— what do YOU know about it?"

If all you're offering up in the poem are nice, general sayings and platitudes, you will lose the reader early on— especially if you use "we." So if you should decide to employ the "we," make sure you've got something original to say, and can say it in a musical, image-filled way. Don't ever bite off more subject matter than: **a)** you can chew; or **b)** a reader will swallow. Selecting the right person to tell the story of your poem is important, since you must decide on it before you begin. When you do, have a good reason why you're using "I," or any other person. If you have the reason, or several, then use it. Dylan Thomas had fine license to use "I" in the splendid "Fern Hill," and of course many other poets, famous and otherwise, have their own. But do think about it. Then write for your reader, not for you. Whichever person you use, if the voice is strong and the craft quietly evident, the reader will find YOU, and you, them.

CAPITAL PUNISHMENT—
THE USE AND MISUSE OF CAPS

Capital letters can be used in different ways, so the only "rule" here would be for the poet to be cognizant of how capitals can be *abused,* and then be CONSISTENT with their application, depending on style. Having just used capitals (caps) to make a sort of bull-horn point of emphasis, this convention obviously has at least one good use. It has others, too.

Use caps to respect your reader. But know there are several ways to respect them, or disrespect them.

By observing the patterns of standard written English you enhance understanding of your poem, even when line breaks continue a sentence down the page. If you are using punctuation to maintain order and comprehension, it's a good idea to use caps with the same intent. This means you use them at BEGINNINGS of actual sentences, and also for proper names, as well as for the pronoun "I." Note here that in poems especially, a complete statement may not show its subject and verb overtly. Yet such elements are *clearly implied* in an independent *elliptical clause,* e.g., Shakespeare's famous "A horse, a horse, my kingdom for a horse!" These statements *count as sentences,* and end with a period. Even when your sentence tumbles several lines down a page, and even if that statement *continues* into a new stanza, don't add a new, "initial" cap until your actual SENTENCE is over.

(An example of the standard use of caps to start individual sentences within a poem follows, as well as an example of an instance where you continue a sentence to a new stanza, and so, don't employ a cap.)

COMMUNION SONATA (excerpt)

She leaves this place
a vacuum of answers
easing the door
behind her.

The ants
move quicker among their blades as she passes,
their feelers to the skyblue air
unthinking.

(Above, caps were only necessary at the beginning of each stanza.)

ATLAS, REVISED

Herzegovina.
Brigadoon, without music.

Borders leach, paper feels the eraser—
the running mascara of skewed lines
tilting, turning, in gall, in godless creed;

mapmaker, throw new dirt into old holes.

*(Here, note that the second strophe [or stanza] did NOT end in a
period; it only "rests" with a semicolon. Therefore, the one-line third
strophe did NOT begin with a capital. That line is part of the previous*

sentence, not a new sentence. Also note that to begin that second poem, I wanted the first two lines to stand alone as individual sentences.)

Now, for those who prefer a less standard poetic form, say in the vein of E. E. Cummings or Frank O'Hara, you're best served by using little or no punctuation if you are also planning to eliminate caps. In other words, strip the poem COMPLETELY of both caps and periods, semicolons, even commas or dashes unless you absolutely need a stronger pause between words or lines (and even then, an extra space or indent can take the comma's or dash's place). This type of poetry thrives on economy. To add any halfhearted punctuation-and-capital convention (although Cummings *did* love parentheses), could ruin the effect for the reader, disengaging him. With caps, it's often *all or nothing.*

All right, what about those proper names? And the word "I"? This time, the jury appears to be out. You could retain those caps and be safe, or again, dispense with caps *entirely.* You could apply one of various schemes, or invent a method all your own. But remember, if the approach is too disjointed (caps only sometimes, punctuation only sometimes) you may end up compromising a reader. As always, you should employ *any* tactic consistently *throughout* your poem.

One more thing— poetry before the last century often enforced the use of a cap to **start each line,** regardless of sentence structure. This convention is as old as poetry is; many poets, including famous ones, still use it today. But beware: a cap beginning a line is a tip-off that a new sentence is beginning, or that the word is a proper noun; so logically, the premise can throw a reader— especially in *short-line* poems. With these, except perhaps to *begin* a lengthy *vertical statement,* as in the work of Williams, you may want to avoid caps at the start of each line.

Now, wait. Blake, Rossetti, Dickinson, even Roethke used first-letter caps on short poems. Doesn't that belie such a warning? Maybe *not.*

I've found that in longer-line poems, especially those in which every clause or phrase doesn't finish predictably on *each line,* the old "first-letter-capped" mode doesn't get in the way. (I don't use this capping approach in my own work; that's just a style preference.) When I read good poems by those who *do* use the setting, I find that I skip over the caps easily, even unconsciously, since poets of worth express ideas freely, and don't confine their thoughts or statements to one line. With *short-line* poems, however, mastery of such capping becomes an *art.*

A new poet, unsure, takes things *a line at a time.* As such, phrasing can be further burdened by caps, and this may stall the reader. If you've just started, do yourself a favor for now. Consider dropping first-letter caps *unless* they begin new sentences, or *unless* they mark proper names.

Can you use caps for startling effect? Suddenly in a middle of a poem go— DIE DOG. Yes, you could, although *not often.* I think I've used that sort of thing once in thirty-five years, and it was to "broadcast" a shout. The truth is, I don't even have the trick in my bag.

Can you start a word with a cap just to emphasize a word that you feel is important? Such as:

> The tide
> binds our Love
> with the Gravity of God.

Well yes, you can. Emily Dickinson did. But Emily lived in the 19th century, when nouns were frequently capitalized; meanwhile, your calendar years start with a "2." Instead, try isolating important words by using *line breaks.* Besides, if you write a good poem, there will be enough impact in the images and language to evoke the importance of "love," "betrayal," or other concepts in the piece, so you don't have to distract anyone with the street sign of capitalization.

And that's about it on caps. Every poet has a style, and may employ caps a variety of ways. Place each according to your dictate— but don't neglect them, and neither, let them command YOU. Readers will thank you for the effort.

AVOIDING BRAND X: TITLES FOR YOUR POEMS

New poets, even working ones, will commonly look at titles as pests or afterthoughts. In reality, the title is a poem's most important line, followed by the first and last. While poets may start with a title, or at least a *topic,* many tag the title on at the end. Either way, think of the title as an essential part of the poem— and that your poem is not only not finished— it is also *compromised* if the right title is not matched to it. Good poems are not generic; they earn their own names.

Whether a title comes early or late in the process of writing the poem, consider it an integral part of the proceedings. The title can be used to point the poem's direction, to add an element of "plot" or atmosphere, to underscore a particular important aspect in a poem, or, as guidepost, to enhance the poem's conclusion or overall impression on the reader.

While a title tagged on early may help the poet focus on his or her subject matter, know that the title is usually easier changed than a major portion of the poem. Often a poet will start with one idea, and by time he or she is finished, the poem has pushed itself into another area, perhaps related but still, a different idea or image-string than that with which the poet began. In such a case, changing the title would be an imperative.

If you have finished a poem and have yet to find a title— DON'T just tag on the first thought that comes to your mind. Read your poem aloud— sit with the poem awhile. Typically, unless a particular line is of tremendous importance and will really, really ring in the reader's ear when they find it again in the poem, avoid taking your title from a phrase within the piece itself. Stay clear of using your title to "tell" too much about the content of the poem, especially the "punch line," or moment of discovery with which most good poems end.

Also, avoid broad concept words ("love," "beauty," "hope," "faith") as a title. Using those or similar nebulous brands implies you have the last word to say on such broad subjects, and even the greatest poets of the ages would not stake that claim. And, such titles don't help the reader. The reader wants to *discover* from what he or she is shown, not *told* with all the subtlety of a club in the back of the head.

If you are using the title to illuminate some aspect of the poem, make your scope of reference as *narrow* as possible. It could require words that reflect quiet simplicity upon an object, a place, a person— some fragment of the whole, rather than the whole itself. The phrase could act as a hint or clue to unlock deeper meaning and direction within the poem's core. If you've lent detail to that particular article in the poem, perhaps you choose a different word or phrase that casts some further light, shade, or perspective on the item. Use your title to *show* even more than the poem showed at its ending. A title should not only set the course for a poem's progress, it should also enlighten the progress, and as well, the conclusion, so that when the title is scanned again at end of the poem's reading, it completes a circle for the reader. In this process, the title becomes at once a password, a sign, or a talisman.

And now, about purposely "untitled" poems. By leaving off the title, a poet is not only cheating himself out of an opportunity to emblazon a work with one deft stroke— he is also making the reader's job more difficult. While early editors *invented* titles for Emily

Dickinson's verses (collected posthumously), and haiku maintains its tradition of *having* no titles— most poems suffer for lack of them. The "untitled" poem, submitted to a prospective editor, could be negating its own consideration. Think of this: how many poems have you seen in fine literary magazines, excepting haiku, that are without titles?

So spend time on this effort. You work so hard on your poem, on getting it right. Why falter at the point of the title? If you stay focused on your work, the title will come— in fact, it could come during the process, like an image rising out of those popular mosaic books. The title's inspiration can actually change or enhance not only the making of the piece, but also the outcome. Treat your poem like the best new secret-ingredient-whiter-than-white detergent on the market— not some "Brand X" that's not worthy of a title to define why it is special, why you wrote it, why the reader must read it, and why, with a little luck and a lot of craft, it may endure thereafter.

Each work is worthy of a great title. If you've done your job as poet— it HAS to be.

POETRY AS MUSIC, MUSIC AS POETRY

I have often told poets privately that they can increase the quality of their work in short order by doing several things that do not involve writing poems. One of them is to listen to music— specifically music that captures the dynamics inherent in all fine poetry, from Shakespeare to Keats, Eliot to Brooks. This dynamic is one of an essential sound and rhythm— something that surpasses the rule of any fixed form or preordained notion of what poetry is.

The fact is, you could hear such poetry, good poetry read in another language, and still know that it is poetry. What you are hearing is the "music"— and it IS music, just as if you were listening to the scored patterns of Mozart, Bach, and Duke Ellington, or the improvisation of Charlie Parker and Ravi Shankar. The arrangement of sounds and their flow, put to paper or freshly performed, transcends the normal demands of rhetoric, or "story." As with the impact of painting, music hits in the gut, or intuitively, upon some super-sense— without further interpretation being necessary. Poetry is another of these arts— and it is this quality that makes it different from prose. True, the *semantic,* or *meaning* aspect of poetry is shared with prose in many instances— but it is the **music** of poetry that sets it apart. Unfortunately, many poets will never get that musical consciousness into their work. As a result, their poems seem dry, rote, formulaic. Rather than pull one's hair out trying to instill the music through merely changing forms, or by *overstressing* sound devices such as rhyme or alliteration, I tell a poet to do the following:

Go to the store. Bring 25 dollars or so. Buy a very well-played set of **Chopin's Nocturnes.** Play them **100 times,** sometimes listening intently, sometimes as background. Do this over a period of months. The poet (and poems) will begin to improve. Lines will become more elastic, rather than stiff (probably more *enjambment* will show up). Meter will become more flexible. (No straight, metronomic iambs any more.) Assonance and consonance will be less forced, but probably more prevalent, as tone colors come out in the form of inter-mingling vowels and consonants. Word choices will improve. Over-all structure, beginning, middle, end, will become smoother, with the poet viewing an entire poetic architecture, rather than struggling to stack line on top of line. Why solo piano music? Why Chopin? Why the nocturnes?

While many types of music could be inspirational in this regard, solo piano lends itself as a remarkably faithful companion to poetic structure. Separate notes can equal words, the chords phrases, the scales or chord sequences can equal lines (or better, *sentences*), entire melodic / harmonic strains, the stanzas, and so forth. It need not be an exact equivalent, but the use of piano, with its maximal octave range and clear intonation seems the best starting point. (Leonard Bernstein, in fact, used this direct comparison in discussing "musical linguistics" during his famous Norton Lectures at Harvard, and the piano was his demonstration instrument.)

Since melody is so important, and Chopin was arguably the world's most innovative melodist, his work is natural to explore. And nowhere does one find such a combination of surface simplicity and fathomless depth— as well as full dynamics of loud / soft, fast / slow, light / dark, as in the nineteen nocturnes (plus two attributed posthumous ones) of Chopin. They are all different, exploring just about all the keys of the scale, and many moods— including moods that shift mid-piece.

Most important when listening (and something you can't grasp as easily looking at the score) is the **rubato,** or stretching of the rhythm as written. This is done as part of the performance interpretation of just about any piece of classical music, and is especially prominent in solo renderings of classical works. The "pulling" that places an accent just before, or just after when it is expected, the slowing down and speeding up, this pulls the listener along, keeping him or her slightly off balance and ever attentive. A fine poet will write such elasticity into the work, and emphasize it in live reading.

There it is. I dare you to invest that 25 dollars in your poetic career and buy the Chopin Nocturnes. Listen to them in the car, at home, in front of you, in the background, even while you sleep. Play them 100 times. *Really, 100 times.* And buy a good version— since the nocturnes can be easily badly played, just as poetry can be badly recited. The versions I would recommend are: Artur Rubinstein on RCA (missing the posthumous Nos. 20 and 21, however), Claudio Arrau on Philips, or Maria João Pires on Decca. These recordings are all masterworks, yet they differ slightly from each other— the overall speeds and that rubato effect, especially. After you have lived with them, and get what I've been saying, you may want to try Scarlatti's keyboard sonatas. These pieces are quite marvelous too, and the next logical step after Chopin. Bach's preludes (really any of his keyboard music), Mozart's piano concertos (the solos and accompaniment), or Beethoven's piano sonatas continue the list; you will pick up different things from each. But try the Chopin first.

Do what I tell you on this. No matter how good a poet you may be at this time, or think you are, you'll thank me some day for this advice. Chopin's Nocturnes. Yes! Do it now!

PIECING IT TOGETHER: THE "CHESS" OF POETRY

This time, another broad analogy, and a possible direction for creating fine poetry, outside of its writing. To develop poems of quality, the poet becomes immersed in a simultaneous offensive and defensive struggle as required in the game of chess. Chess, like poetry is an exercise in creativity, study, intuition, rules and patterns of progress. A poem must have a clear beginning, middle, and end, one building to the next, inexorably. Anyone who plays decent chess knows it is the same there. There must be, as in poetry, not only a grand strategy, but also adept tactics as play moves forward. And as in chess, the poet pores over hundreds of *poems,* as his wary counterpart does *games,* in order to integrate his own and others' past forays (including those of the great masters), to learn from each, yet create a style and unique paths to success. For the poet, what must be overcome? Like Bobby Fischer playing many boards in simultaneous exhibitions, there may be a multiplicity of hurdles— rules, durations, expectation, data flows, old and new understandings, twists of logic— in fact, all manner of problems, not least of which is the confidence and preparedness of oneself. In order to win, a poet must be ready to confront them all.

Does the poet have or at any moment retain the knowledge of ALL the rules and possible moves of the game, and their intricacies? Does he or she have not only the basic knowledge to start a game, but also knowledge in patterns of attack and defense (ebb and flow, daring-do or dutiful convention), combined with the various lines and alterations of those lines that can turn a game in a different direction, caused by either a brilliant inspiration on the part of the poet, or the threat of a particular obstacle that falls in the path?

What of those rules and logics? In poetry, beyond basic grammar and usage, comes retention of an available vocabulary that grows with experience of actual use in speech, not just out of a dictionary. What is OK to use, and when? Does one have three word choices there, or thirty-three? Whatever the number claimed, how many are actually *appropriate* words, or correct *definitions* for the context? And which one is *perfect?* Are the words or idioms overused, or archaic? Does the poet use a "big" word when a small one will do? Will the choice destroy a line, kill momentum, dictate disaster? If the poet follows a particular mode, is he or she attacking blindly, to succeed or fail in a flash, or is the poet plodding along, in a pedestrian and predictable manner, word by word, line by line? Can the poet / player stay clear of such potentially hazardous extremes, win the center of the board, and so assure victory?

There is so much there. For instance, if the poet writes a narrative, or story-based poem, will he or she be drawn into the boggy slog of sequential past tense, without the vibrance of present-time dialogue, face *padded lines* to feed details of that narrative, get strangled in *too-predictable metric-feet* or fearfully sate the dictates of the meter at the expense of clarity? Will the poet be so careful and fussy as to turn the poem into prose? Will the poet know how to bring the poem to its logical conclusion, and make the moves at the latter part, the endgame, that will force the *great finish,* the mate? Will the poet push the poem to such *unnecessary length* that he bores the reader, ending the game at a draw? Or will a chopped, impulsive free verse be too obtuse, too difficult to follow, and so do the same? Finally, will the poet use his or her ego to move ahead, to take chances, and yet control that ego so as not to overlook a killer mistake? Everywhere, the poet, as the player, struggles with the moves, the lines, the history of an exalted game.

There is much drama in a chess match, and just as much drama (or there should be) in the writing of a poem. Think about that as you write. As the great chess player plans and assesses his or her pattern of play, as well as an opponent's, *five, even ten moves ahead,* so must the poet build the poem— not just word by word, not even line by line, but section by section, seeing a wider and wider scope of the game-board and its pieces if any prize is to be gained. And the greater the ambition of the construction, in this case of recurring metaphors or sound patterns, the more difficult the challenges of adaptation, and of self-correction. All that said, is there still room for slapdash flair, for a swashbuckling defiance of convention? Yes, there is— but only if the poet is so well grounded in craft, in the rules of the language, and what sonic and rhythmic devices require that he can carefully *break those rules* without ruin. In the end, *that's* what it's all about, what we all strive for. It is that transcendent capability that separates in the chess world a Fischer, Tal, or Alekhine from the pack, just as it separates a Keats, a Yeats, or a Williams in our poetic zone.

This is a noble thing we do, writing poetry. And it is the truth—beginner or grandmaster—we have the same tools or pieces, the same board, the same independent creativity, the same capacity for work. At least, all that potential is there in every one of us. With study and practice, with trial and error, with experience and encouragement of others who have traveled the ranks and files, of those who have seen seemingly every square and permutation of the board, we write poetry. And we have our kindred among the chess players of this world, who toil in a quiet, raging logic, a beautiful, calculated sort of madness, playing a game that is more than a game, just as we do. For each Paul Morphy, a Hart Crane. For each Kasparov, a Stevens, a Jeffers, a Plath. It is a quest, public or private, with the power to consume.

Chess and poetry go together. I play the annotated games of Fischer out on a chessboard just as I read Auden or Yeats, or, as I wrote about before, listen to the nocturnes of Chopin. All these sources are instructive, all are inspirational. Play them, study them, learn from them. They are, as I have struggled to articulate here, symbiotic. Go ahead, set up the pieces, scan the board— employ both mind and intuition. **Find five reasons** why you used that word, that line, that stanza, just as the chess player has five reasons why he moved that particular pawn, or knight, or rook— even if those reasons flashed as seconds' prelude to the moving of the piece, driven by experience, by instinct, by wild ironies, and for love of the game.

BEYOND THE LINES: BEGINNING, MIDDLE, AND END

Poems are not just lines. Repeat— poems are NOT just lines.

Stop writing just lines. Instead, let's talk about building something with them.

The young or inexperienced poet writes *in lines, only.* Goaded by the dictates of end-rhymed or otherwise fixed meter, or simple lack of vision in free verse, this poet's scope confines itself to writing the line at hand. That line could be at the beginning, middle, or end of the poem. It doesn't matter. *And it's a GREAT line!* (Consider *framing* it.) The line comes from nothing, from no plan; and it contributes to nothing, to no real outcome. Just lines. Such lines, however clustered into a general look, if not substance of a poem, could have something to do with courage, or love, or a cat, or Madame Curie, or the beach. Or unfortunately, ALL those things. If the scope of a poem does not extend beyond *a line at a time,* the first line won't lead to the second, or the fifty-sixth, ultimately, to the eightieth. In other words, it's not really a poem— it's a passel of unmatched, unplugged *lines.* Hey, they may even rhyme—but they're *still* just a bunch of lines.

A poems consists of statements which could take in one line, or six, or twenty, or two hundred, managed in downward flow by the mechanics of poetic device, and achieved within a relatively normal framework of grammar and usage. Sure, a poem can have several, or many commas, semicolons, or spaces, continuing that thought which does not yet require the full stop of a period. But the poet must know that a poem is a *statement,* however broad, enclosing *other* statements within itself. The line, like the words, and even the syllables of the words, plus punctuation or space, are simply the mortar and brick, rafters or thatch of the building, a construction. The statements are *WHO live and breathe inside the building.* And just as you usually can't describe people or ideas with one catch-all line, neither can you forward a poem that way. You must think bigger. You must plan, you must adapt to obstacles, and you must see this undertaking through to its conclusion.

You start at the **beginning.**

Now, the beginning is almost always *not* your title. Titles have other uses. (See the previous chapter on **titles**.) They hint at the core of your poem, or color a little something the reader will see later, making that article or element far more important than it might have been.

It is your **first statement** that is so very important. If you falter here, like a sprinter stumbling out of the blocks, you will never catch up. Remember, too, that this statement can take up *more* than one line. It may contain both clauses and phrases commanding several lines, even several stanzas. Here you open a door, creating quickly some view— an image, an action, something that will build and build upon itself as the poem moves along. You may tantalize at the beginning, showing a direction you'll go, but not indicating the destination. That destination you will spell out, or keep close to you. Sometimes, the direction can change slightly, or more than slightly, as you decide to take one exit off the highway instead of the next— still, you know that either way should get you home. Oh, don't forget if you should take the longer of the two— *a reader* is sitting alongside you. Make the trip worthwhile; show your front-seat rider the sights!

Poems are more often than not the unraveling of some mystery, large or small. In the beginning, you lay out a piece of the puzzle. In the middle, you enlarge and elaborate on it. The **middle** is the section for elaboration, or for turning. The reader here gets a full measure of something that was previously fragmentary, and with that perhaps, is turned in a slightly different direction than that which was thought to be the way. Mind you, DON'T introduce brand new subject matter— work off what you have. If you find yourself introducing some other subject, you'll have to really work to tie that subject in. As that arises, consider that you're not in the middle of a poem— you're STILL at the beginning, and probably will have a long poem on your hands!

Unfortunately, long poems easily become disordered assemblies, out of-control "mansions" for which our intrepid builders lost the plans— Chinese Modern sitting room here; Hemingway's rustic den, shotgun and moose head over the mantel, there. Be aware that if you find yourself shifting subjects, and those subjects are not *artfully tied to the main theme* and designed to *forward the poem* to its finish— you are actually making OTHER POEMS— *not* the one you were working on. Certain lines, even whole stanzas (in free verse, irregular-lined stanzas or verse-units are called **strophes**), can burn with their own lambent beauty, and yet be totally out of agreement with the direction of your poem. Don't worry, you will use those seeming sacred lines, stanzas, or strophes later— SAVE THEM. But get them out of *that* poem!

At times, a lot of times, poets don't know how to **end** their poems. A decent general rule is that a poem should end with the reader, who has changed somehow along with the poem, gaining that *ooooh, aaaah,* or *knowing smile* of resolution— in other words, coming to a point of personal discovery through the use of logic, humor, emotion, or irony. It's an end that should seem to have arrived in a specially inevitable way; the reader receives a *punch line.* Its ultimate success, however, will depend on how you labored to that final statement, always tying what you show and express back to the ring of previous statements, and always foreshadowing what will come. Also, the ending should play distinctively on the ear. If you're rhyming, let it be just a *great* rhyme— natural, original, a perfect fit. Whatever the fixed form or scheme, you must have built to *that* moment.

At the same time, the sound of a free verse ending is just as important. You might use rhyme here, either vowel rhyme or the subtle "rhyme" of consonance that goes back several lines into the text for delayed effect. You could inlay alliterative grace notes, swell as brass might, or adjourn with some soft kiss, depending on the poem. Remember, not all great pieces of music resolve with a crescendo (although the majority do, and many patrons perched in balconies expect it). Some poems rather cry for the taken risk, for a decision, having fired off all bombast already, to end quietly.

Either way, your ending has to fall naturally, as if of its own accord. A poem can finish in three lines, in thirty, in a hundred. Eventually, you'll gain the ability to let the poem tell you when it's over. It will, if you listen. But you must stand vigil on an ending, inspect it carefully, and assure confidence in the entire project. It's only then, when it's over that you'll know you're really home, off the byways and settled into a strong house, with all the lights on, in the warm charm of your very best guests.

THE ALCHEMY OF JUXTAPOSITION: POETRY ON THE NEXT LEVEL

One of the most effective creative directions I have seen for poets comes from an exercise casually mentioned in Michael J. Bugeja's book, *The Art and Craft of Poetry* (Writer's Digest Books). Inviting a tremendous leap for some, should they truly *get* what Bugeja, an excellent poet and teacher is talking about— and upon which I've both paraphrased and elaborated here— the idea is this:

*Think of someone— say, a banker. Consider everything about him, what describes him, his tools of the trade, etc. Once you have a good description in your mind, take the banker and drop him in an unlikely place— Bugeja, brilliantly, offers a **rainforest**. Now write your poem.*

What we're getting at is mastering use of a fine tool with which any poet can empower themselves and their readers: it's the **juxtaposition of subjects.** Now, the idea here is *not* to wander off to an entirely new, *isolated* subject— a careless placement of material that we had stated you should guard *against*. Rather, we mean the playing of one spool of subject matter *on and off another,* like winding together red and gold thread. We saw previously that *metaphor* enables a poet to work in and around an unfamiliar reader, surpassing statements that require and gain only a surface agreement or disagreement— the usual "black and white." Similarly, a *purposeful* juxtaposition and blend of usually unrelated subjects frames viewpoint in a unique way. Done well, it is at least, interesting. Done really well, it gives poet and reader a much deeper connection than occurs in clichés aimed at the mass audience, and copied into popular songs, greeting cards, or other offshoots of what is called— great adjective— "occasional poetry."

Always look to tell a story, or paint a scene a different way. By fusing two disparate subjects or scenes (here, the banker and the rainforest), you arrive right away at metaphor possibilities of two specific classes. Hence, the metaphors you use should not stray; instead, these phrases twist in a unique, yet well-defined scope, and follow each other with a sense of building. What might a banker do to a rainforest, or with one? What might a rainforest do with *him,* our banker? Well, the banker could "mortgage the air with chainsaws" (an eco-political poem in the works), or the rainforest could "water a dry ledger, with dividends of dahlias to show." Who knows where the poem goes— since you have two distinct sets of subjects, images, or details from which to draw.

Perhaps some of my best poems, or at least, the best-published, came astride an opportune power afforded by such juxtapositions— from the risky extended metaphors that John Donne and his Metaphysical poets called *conceits.* In a long poem titled "John of Revelation at the Rose Parade," I compared religion with popular culture, making John from the Book of Revelation a broadcast "color man" at the Tournament of Roses Parade. This created ample metaphor possibilities, including constructing flower-laden floats out of Bible prophecy, and 144,000 "chosen people" heading for the Rose Bowl and "the game."

"Anne Sexton" is an elegy for a great poet with whom I had planned to study— just before she took her own life. In the poem, I inserted myself amid allusions to *The Wizard of Oz*— while bending one of the film's signatures—blending "I (believe) I'll miss you most of all" with the line "friends passing by the window, Lowell harnessed to his baggage, Sylvia on her Schwinn..." and the ironies of "Finally, you let me safely down," and "Black-and-white turns October technicolor..." Of course, I was writing about personal regret, about loss, not about

The Wizard of Oz. It's the same with you. You will use such tools of juxtaposition to make your poems flash with vision, with originality, and with the power to move. And since you're in control of what subjects and scenes you combine (not to mention, as below, effects like a subtly disconcerting gender inversion that begins with the opening simile), you will have great fun indulging in this alchemy. Lead can become gold, when you try.

ANNE SEXTON

I'm like Dorothy, lining up for the balloon ride.
Dearest Anne, my vehicle of some emulation,
I believe I'll miss you most of all, but wait—

must I leave you behind, can't I sit with you
in the carriage, listening to soft radio, until
the shovel hung and plant-stakes turn to clouds,

turn to puffiest clouds of ether, or forgetfulness
and you could give me all those special lessons,
introduce me to your fey fire, your insouciance,

your friends passing by the window, Lowell harnessed
to his baggage, Sylvia on her Schwinn, Betsy Bishop
vodka-toasting a circle of the circle's shrinks

who wash their blood-hands of invisible ink, as I fish
for a match to hold under them, looking for passwords
to reclaim a thousand artists' souls— yours, too.

I'd like to think I would have been the one ingenue
of your unschooled, oh-so-wicked way to penetrate
and hold you fast, to steer you to the fast winds

eliminating the rowing toward God, and on green air
or water lilt and undulate, letting you seduce me
in a way that would offend no one, responding with psalms.

Instead, you would let me safely down. And I,
confused, took a twenty-year day job, writing on the sly,
and wondering, if I could have been with you then, would I?

Through all the pain, the poems sing back to me—
"So open the garage door, will you, hon?" And I do.
Black-and-white turns October technicolor, and every time

some Dorothy's pen treads paper, so do you.

THE FORMS OF POETRY: PART ONE—
METERS, FEET, AND LINES

Poets so often get hung up trying to learn, or "remember," the **forms** of poetry. You'll note that I avoided talking too much about forms in past chapters, no doubt to the puzzlement of eager new poets. But it is far more important for a poet to master poetic sensibility before addressing the fixed forms of centuries of English and world poetry. That means learning and using in all manner of experiment— aligned with hard practice— the art of sound recognition and the use of sound, the weapon of metaphor, and the extension of English grammar and syntax into the tight, essential world of verse. After that, the "forms" of poetry, both fixed and traditional, or otherwise radical and new, can fuse a poet's message into a light all readers can follow with profit, and without, hopefully, having the bloody torch shined in their eyes. And on that note, we begin the discussion of **FORMS.**

TYPES OF METER

We introduced the general subject before; here's a bit more for you. **Meter** is the *measure* of a poem's lines. The line can be measured by:

1) syllable count, a construction called **SYLLABIC METER**— no undue weight is given to any syllable, and there is no reliance on vocal stresses wherever they may naturally appear.

2) beats, or strong-sounded stresses, a primarily **aural** construction called **ACCENTUAL METER**— it is normally arrayed in patterns of **vocal stresses or accents,** as in early Anglo-Saxon poetry. Read a line aloud, naturally, and you **hear** the stresses. A return to reliance on spoken-word accents has been promoted by various "modern" poets going back a century or more; cowboy poetry, rap / hip-hop and other types of performance poetry are recent, pure examples of it. But lines of poetry are most *often* measured by:

3) a combination of *both* **accented and unaccented syllables** made into **poetic feet**, called **ACCENTUAL-SYLLABIC METER**. A **foot** is a group of syllables arrayed in a measurable pattern, consisting of **stressed** (accented) syllables, and their attached, **unstressed** syllables— the written equivalent to a bar of composed music. This meter usually, but not always, focuses on counted sequences of the weak-then-strong foot known as the **iamb.** Accentual-syllabic meter has been, by far, the most prevalent of meters employed in English poetry over the last six hundred years. It uses both visual and aural recognition of words and sounds in a greater or lesser balance.

CONSTRUCTION OF FEET AND LINES

Poems in fixed meter contain lines with sets of: weak syllables, strong accented ones, and in combination, those measured rhythmic patterns called *feet*. There may be the same number of feet in each line, or the poet could arrange new and different patterns of lines or stanzas, with still-preordained numbers of feet within each *set* of lines. Except for free verse, most of the modern poetry that you'll read, and much of the romantic poetry you remember from school is based, as we stated, on a fixed *combination* of syllables and stresses per line that we call *accentual-syllabic meter.*

Such meter follows a specific, overall plan, and much of it is built around a weak (unstressed)-then-strong (stressed) pattern of syllables in each foot. (Once again, that type of foot is called *iambic*, using the *iamb.*) A line's pattern can be set very "regular" (all weak / strong "iambic" feet), or it can be varied to include other types of feet, with additional syllables added to or subtracted from some feet before OR after a stress. (More on the many **types of feet** below.)

The total number of strong stresses, or "beats" in a line (you can count them off with your hand) could be one, two, three, four, five, or even six beats (or more). The stresses are important in finding the *audible length* of the meter, and in guiding what the listener or reader absorbs.

But what of the other syllables in the line that add to both sound and rhythm? On one level, the combination of stressed and unstressed syllables appear visually *equal* on the page; as such, literary poetry (based on accentual-syllabic meter) took firm hold, following the available, mass-produced order the invention of the printing press afforded. Of course, the *silent* reader "hears" what he reads, too, as if being read to by the poet. Thus, the reader *does* note all the "vocal" stresses, and as such, we have the sliced-and-diced complications of English prosody.

In any event, the number of **stresses** (beats) AND their **unstressed syllables** are laid out this way in feet:

Monometer: (one foot to a line)
Dimeter: (two feet to a line)
Trimeter: (three feet to a line)
Tetrameter: (four feet to a line
Pentameter: (five feet to a line)
Hexameter [also called **Alexandrine**]: (six feet to a line)
Heptameter: (seven feet to a line)
Octameter: (eight feet to a line), and so on...

The most common line length used is **pentameter,** with the slightly shorter **tetrameter** coming in a distant second— the latter lending its length to many of the simplest, sweetest poems you first learned. The combinations of *iambic* **pentameter** and *iambic* **tetrameter** are relied on to arrange most form-based poetic lines— probably since, if you're going to instill order in written poetry that others (both readers and writers) may follow, these foot-types reflect poetic rhythms closest to the speech patterns of Norman-infused English, French, and Italian. This does not mean that *all* the feet in a line have to have that iambic weak / strong configuration, unless the poet intends it. But a majority of feet in most lines will tend to be of that construction, and when measuring and marking meter, a process called **scansion**, lines are often tested for adherence to the orderly predominance of iambs.

Given variations of *vocal emphasis* one finds in any spoken line of English, it's hard to *count out* (da DUH, da DUH) *ALL iambs* in order to maintain strict *iambic* tetrameter, pentameter, hexameter, etc.) The audible stresses (beats) may actually accrue to *less* than the number of feet planned. But as scanned, even it doesn't sound entirely natural, it's considered to be "iambic" meter. (Sometimes, you'll even see an extra weak syllable added to the start of a line, or one hacked off at the end, and tacit agreement says, "no problem.") Within the process of writing, the poet must decide whether to lean to the natural vocal stress, or to the dictate of "iambic order." Often, there's compromise.

The fact is, all types of feet can be inserted to make the poem flow one way or another, or to alter the sometime monotony of *too many* audible iambs. Also, you can base a poem partly or entirely on some of these other types of rhythmic feet. **Here's a list of them**— a weak syllable expressed as "da," a stressed syllable (or beat), as "DUH."

iambic, iamb (da DUH) we FLY

monosyllabic foot (DUH) SHOOT!

trochaic, trochee (DUH da) MONster

spondaic, spondee (DUH DUH) CANEBRAKE

anapestic, anapest (da da DUH) to a MAN

dactylic, dactyl (DUH da da) SUCcubus

pyrrhic (da da, with no stress attached) [pyrrhic in brackets]
the CAMel's LIFE [is a] DREARry ONE

hypermetrical (an extra, uncounted "da" after a stress at end of line)
[hypermetrical in brackets] to MISS, or BE withOUT a SIS [ter]

amphibrach (da DUH da) stuPENDous

amphimacer (DUH da DUH) CHARing CROSS

tribrach (da da da) [tribrach in brackets] ON[ly to be] DASHED;

molussus (DUH DUH DUH) COLD GRAY STONES

bacchius (da DUH DUH) paZUZU

antibacchius (DUH DUH da) STILL WET the

ionic (either da da DUH DUH) polyPHEMUS (or DUH DUH da da)
HIPPOlyta

Natural Rhythm and Emphasis, Versus Planned Meter:

Rhythmic sound of any kind, including speech and its encoding into
script, may be natural, or planned. *Meter* measures rhythm and en-
forces order, whether at the audible surface, or beneath it; but rhythm
always exists, and is part of natural speech. Because of those welcome
beats, ***accentual meter*** rises to challenge the dominance of ***accentual-
syllabic meter.*** "The majority" however, has long enforced the latter
design, one that clusters weak and strong syllables into units in order
to control and perhaps color the poetry, creating *subliminal* timbre as a
vibrating reed separates a clarinet from a recorder— thus assuring our
reliance on English accentual-syllabic meter, and its measurable *feet*.

FORMS: PART TWO— THE SONNET: 14 LINES ON A MUSIC STAND

It's at once the most revered, maligned, abused, exalted and exasperating form in all of poetry. It's the form English teachers select for parsing. The famous ones are memorized— the template branded on the psyche of poets professing an unlikely vocation. And there are more of these poems around— great, good, bad and godawfully bad, than there are dandelions in an unkept cemetery. Yes— we're talking about **the sonnet.** 19th century poet Dante Gabriel Rossetti, who along with sister Christina, penned hundreds of them, remarked:

> A Sonnet is a moment's monument,—
> Memorial from the Soul's eternity
> To one dead deathless hour. Look that it be,
> Whether for lustral rite or dire portent
> Of its own intricate fullness reverent:
> Carve it in ivory or in ebony,
> Day or Night prevail; and let Time see
> Its flowering crest impearled and orient.
>
> A Sonnet is a coin: its face reveals
> The soul,— its converse, to what Power 'tis due:—
> Whether for tribute to the august appeals
> Of Life, or dower in Love's high retinue
> It serve; or, 'mid the dark wharf's cavernous breath
> In Charon's palm it pay the toll to Death.

Yes, for Rossetti, sonnets were serious business. Yet the sonnet carries with it many of the basic conventions and motivations for which poets write poems. And it is the reason that sonneteers tend to linger in this particular form. Well, to linger is not to loiter, lest one be picked up for no means of support. What *are* those basics? How does the poet meet the sonnet's lure, and fulfill its promise?

ATTRIBUTES OF THE SONNET

It is compact— 14 lines. But, Rossetti agrees, a sonnet traffics in the lustre of its own reason, in its musical universe, in its slice of— *Life.*

By allusion, the sonnet carries what is considered the most pristine and logical scheme in music— SONATA form— its parts a sequence of theme and exposition, variation, recapitulation, and coda, resulting in, one hopes, *transformation* of the listener / reader. (Liszt wrote solo piano pieces after Petrarch's sonnets, reciprocating this idea.) Surely, sonnets do require a *composer's* inspiration, his discipline, an ear of perfect pitch, and a staff on which to hang scales, and measure bars.

Our sonnet, however, allows, no, *encourages* the daring poet to push its boundaries, since innovating *within* this form has come to highlight the greatest sonnets ever written. Such features includes the variation-on-theme we mentioned, reverberant harmonics appended to a melody (both as sound and symbolic reference), the occasionally suspended bar-line, sinuous rhythms (something other than iambs), a surprising point, perhaps, of perfect dissonance, then the wry agreement, and at end, that moment of utter transience, and clarity.

When written badly, it is horrendous. When written well, it is more than you could possibly ask for. It's a lot, the sonnet— so don't take it lightly, or you'll deserve the derision that you face in folly of its neglect. Now that we've said all that— yes NOW, and not a minute earlier, we'll give you some classic recipes— just remember that your endeavors strive to make ambrosia, not corn muffins, and music that demands pure listening, not cocktail mingling.

TYPES OF SONNETS

Sonnets have fourteen lines arrayed in a fixed pattern of end-rhymes. (Yeats, Auden, et. al, relaxed the rhyme order.) The major foot-type is *iambic* (da DUH); the meter is *pentameter* (five feet); tetrameter (four feet) is occasionally seen, as in Alexander Pushkin's *Eugene Onegin.*

Actually, many poets believe that a sonnet form, as long as it contains some or all of the other standard sonnet attributes such as line count, regular meter, and a "turn" that we'll cover in a bit, does not have to rhyme, but a sonnet usually does, and in the several forms covered in this book, it always does.

The poem is divided, not only in form, but also in contemplation of meaning as the piece unfolds through its parts and their intended roles. The first eight lines are called the **octave,** the last six, the **sestet.** In the **English (Shakespearean) Sonnet,** there are three four-line stanzas called **quatrains**, and one two-line stanza called a **couplet.** Now, this can be a bit of deceiving labeling, in that these stanzas (and including the couplet at the end) are usually brought together as a single block of text. (Often, though, the end couplet will be indented.)

In the **Italian, or Petrarchan Sonnet,** there are two **quatrains,** followed by two trios of lines, called **tercets.** Flexible, the tercets can be taken into different rhyme schemes according to the poet's direction.

Spot the differences in the rhyming patterns among the three major sonnet forms.

IMPORTANT NOTE:

*In describing the rhyme scheme of a poem, each new and **different** end-rhyme, along with rhyming mates that follow in later lines, will share the **same letter** in the scheme's coded pattern, going through the alphabet (**a, b, c...**) in sequence, with unrhymed lines marked **x**.*

	ENGLISH (Shakespearean)	ITALIAN (Petrarchan)				SPENSERIAN	
Octave	a	a	a	a	a	a	Quatrain
	b	b	b	b	b	b	
	a	b	b	b	b	a	
	b	a	a	a	a	b	
	c	a	a	a	a	b	Quatrain
	d	b	b	b	b	c	
	c	b	b	b	b	b	
	d	a	a	a	a	c	
Sestet	e	Tercet c	c	c	c	c	Quatrain
	f	d	d	d	d	d	
	e	e	c	c	c	c	
	f					d	
	g	Tercet c	d	d	e	e	Couplet
		d	c	d	d		
	g	e	d	c	c	e	

Of the three types of sonnets listed, one can see why the **English, or Shakespearean Sonnet** would be the most prevalent form found IN ENGLISH. This is due largely to veneration accorded William Shakespeare's massive opus of 154 sonnets. *As an aside, not all of these sonnets are as incredibly good as some others, but each in its way is still valuable. In the field of music, a parallel can be drawn to Beethoven's 32 immortal piano sonatas, or to Scarlatti's sonatas-in-miniature, a monumental 555.*

Example, from Shakespeare:

SONNET 18

Shall I compare thee to a summer's day?
Thou art more lovely and more temperate:
Rough winds do shake the darling buds of May,
And summer's lease hath all too short a date:
Sometime too hot the eye of heaven shines,
And often in his gold complexion dimm'd;
And every fair from fair sometime declines,
By chance, or nature's changing course untrimm'd;
But thy eternal summer shall not fade,
Nor lose possession of that fair thou ow'st,
Nor shall death brag thou wander'st in his shade,
When in eternal lines to time thou grow'st;
　So long as men can breathe, or eyes can see,
　So long lives this, and this gives life to thee.

The **Italian, or Petrarchan Sonnet** is also popular, in fact, the most popular *worldwide,* and that's as it should be—since it was the form from which all sonnets originally came, back in the fourteenth century. As the diagram on Page 102 shows, the Italian gives the poet several elective rhyme schemes that may complete the poem. (Petrarch, the style's eventual namesake, and Dante made these famous.)

Example, John Milton:

ON HIS BEING ARRIVED TO THE AGE OF TWENTY-THREE

How soon hath Time, the subtle thief of youth,
Stolen on his wing my three and twentieth year!
My hasting days fly on with full career,
my late spring no bud or blossom shew'th.
Perhaps my semblance might deceive the truth,
That I to manhood am arrived so near,
And inward ripeness doth much less appear,
That some more timely-happy spirits indu'th.
Yet be it less or more, or soon or slow,
It shall be still in strictest measure even
To that same lot, however mean or high,
Toward which Time leads me, and the will of Heaven.
All is, if I have grace to use it so,
As ever in my great Task-master's eye.

The **Spenserian Sonnet,** which is still *English* in origin, and which carries a different style than the other forms, is attributed to the poet Edmund Spenser. It is less widely seen today, but was an antecedent to the *Shakespearian,* that which has become synonymous with the *English Sonnet.* (Remember that you need not be daunted by any of these formats. Rossetti wasn't. If you scrutinize the opening sonnet, he blends elements of *all three styles.* Moral: dare to be different!)

In the meantime, back to the orthodox. Below is a true *Spenserian* Sonnet from its master, Spenser:

SONNET 75

One day I wrote her name upon the strand,
   But came the waves and washed it away:
   Again I wrote it with a second hand,
   But came the tide, and made my pains his prey.
Vain man, said she, that doest in vain assay
   A mortal thing so to immortalize,
   For I myself shall like this to decay,
   And eek my name be wiped out likewise.
Not so (quoth I), let baser things devise
   To die in dust, but you shall live by fame:
   My verse your virtues rare shall eternize,
   And in the heavens write your glorious name.
   Where whenas Death shall all the world subdue,
   Our love shall live, and later life renew.

More important than all this substructure for dictated rhyming is the concept of thematic set-up, variation, and release the sonnet embodies. In a sonnet the octave, the first eight lines, sets the scene or idea. At just that "mid" point, called the **volta,** the scene or idea "turns" in some way (just as most musical compositions do, and all sonatas do), leading the reader to a conclusion, ultimately defined in the **closing couplet** of the sestet.

At this point, we have gone far from where we started in the octave, but not so far that we can't see where we came from. In fact, nowhere in poetry should the "ah!" quotient we like to see on a poem's ending be as naturally profound as in the sonnet— considering the plan of **building** over the octave, **transforming** at the volta, and **resolving** in the sestet. So important is this process that if you haven't paid attention to it, you may not have written a sonnet at all— just, instead, a bad rhyming poem with fourteen lines.

To write a good sonnet, you cast an incisive statement about life, or people, or ideas, upon a shifting apparatus, setting out to transform one particular scenario into another, that ultimate statement which you *really* wanted to get across all along. If you like, look at this form as a simile: THIS is this (*octave*), BUT HEY! (*volta*), we can also make it look like THAT (the *sestet,* and inevitable closing *couplet*). When you can deliver such a comparison, plus vary your pentameter (or tetrameter) and perhaps play artfully with some well-considered, singing rhymes— you'll be writing *sonnets.* The real kind.

And if you're going to write them, then prepare for an exploration— of form yes, music too, but more, much more, of transformation— of the lines, of your reader, and maybe even, of you.

FORMS: PART THREE— THE VILLANELLE

*IMPORTANT NOTE: Just as repeated end-rhymes are coded with sequential letters of the alphabet, the formula for use of **repeated lines** in any poem (as in the **villanelle, pantoum, triolet, rondeau, etc.,** to follow), is denoted by CAPITALIZING the letters involved.*

A villanelle has nineteen lines, five three-line stanzas followed by one four-line stanza, usually in lines of either all tetrameter (4 beats) or all pentameter (5 beats), with interlacing end-rhymes patterned **aba, aba, aba, aba, abaa,** but with one other, vital twist. The first and third lines of the poem actually *alternate* as the last line of stanzas 2, 3, and 4, and then end stanza 5, and the poem itself, as a *couplet*. That rhyme scheme, with the pair of REPEATED lines that *ALSO RHYME*, amends the pattern to: **A1bA2, abA1, abA2, abA1, abA2, abA1A2.** Almost chess notation! But it comes out looking like this:

PRE-RAPHAELITES

Beauty clouds by accident and surprise
rendering malignant flaw from images benign
like the sliver in Fra Lippo Lippi's eye.

In tempera, forms the icon we surmise
awash with cherubs on a barrel-lid of brine—
beauty clouds by accident, and surprise.

Sculpting virgins out of marble, pieces fly,
the resolute and earnest strike resigns
like the sliver in Fra Lippo Lippi's eye.

A crease, a curve, soft to sight, it lies
somewhere between a rhythm and a rhyme—
beauty clouds by accident, and surprise.

But you, bright love, who set yourself astride,
my head within your hands, you drift in kind
like the sliver in Fra Lippo Lippi's eye.

You know, too well, an artist knows he dies
in increments of stone and paint, refined—
beauty clouds by accident, and surprise
like the sliver in Fra Lippo Lippi's eye.

Two of the most famous villanelles, also in pentameter, are Dylan Thomas's "Do Not Go Gentle into That Good Night" and William Empson's "Missing Dates." (Empson wrote many villanelles, and was a master of the form.)

Just as the sonnet's core was the "turn" of the poem's direction or meaning after the first eight lines, the villanelle, another fixed form with patterned rhyme, relies heavily on a specific artifice— that of the *two repeated lines.* These lines, even as they are repeated, change in both position and meaning through the poem, increasing in irony until the final couplet fairly shimmers with this special substance. In that sense, the villanelle is first cousin to the sonnet, not in rhyme scheme or construction per se, but definitely in intent to be something more than at first it seems.

Villanelles are NOT easy to write *well,* and the reason is not so much the meter, the repetition, or the rhyme. It's the difficulty of building the *repeated message's impact* high enough and clear enough, as it weaves itself into and off of supporting lines, without drowning in the poem's inherently complicated "form." Rather, lines must join to challenge the form, enhance it, complete it. Most attempted villanelles fail to do that; it is the part that cannot be copied, only created.

The **two repeating lines** of the villanelle have to be exceptionally strong, or the villanelle will be terrible. If you don't have that strong core couplet— really the center of your poetic thought— you don't have a villanelle— you just have something (similar to our view on form-faithful but failed *sonnets*) in "villanelle style." You must work to make a couplet that can stand the strain— one that may elicit two, even *several* different shades of meaning, depending on how they are raised and turned by the poem's supporting lines. As with sonnets and other rhymed forms, find good, natural rhymes or off-rhymes to complete the scheme, and let the poem flow— don't force anything.

If the couplet is really strong, and you build on it throughout the poem, you could have something about which to be proud. Otherwise, you might become the target for a well-flung custard pie. Dessert anyone? Like the sonnet, a villanelle is not just a "rhymed, metered form." It is a well-planned and musical slice of piercing, honest philosophy, a piece of life, a part of you, and maybe me, and is only incidently clever.

FORMS: PART FOUR— THE BALLAD

The **ballad** form, simple on its face, is ever-present in poetry. This ***verse form*** (it can be used in long poems or short ones) alternates lines of *four feet* (hinged on four stressed syllables or beats) with lines of *three feet*. The lines are often arranged into four-line stanzas, but not always. The feet are sometimes iambic (weak / strong), but don't have to be. When lines *are* largely iambic, they frequently end with a lone stress (essentially a trochee whose weak syllable is allowably cut off). Other times, the lines may be dominated by trochees (strong / weak), and again, the last weak syllable of a line may be cropped. What I'm saying here is that ballads tend to be metrically flexible, and actually lean more heavily on *accents* than on feet.

Whatever the setting, these 4-3-4-3 line arrays make a lilting cadence that lends itself to sweet, or bittersweet, poetry. Surviving eras, it has proven a sturdy scaffold for poems little and big, simple and grand. The tension-then-release, almost "slinky-toy" approach is, in fact, a song form. More than half the songs you listen to on the radio are ballads— even many where the beat is speeded up well beyond its deliberative roots in story-based, English folk music. To use a classic example of the form, consider this ending of the famous folk song, "Mary Hamilton." Mary is a lady-in-waiting at the Queen's court, whose life must be sacrificed because of a discovered tryst with the King. (The stresses, or beats, are capitalized.)

last NIGHT - there WERE - four MA RYS	4 beats
to NIGHT - there'll BE - but THREE	3 beats
there was MA - ry BEAT- on and MA - ry SEA ton	4 beats
and MA - ry car MI - chael and ME	3 beats

Note there that not all the feet are iambic, if you were even going to *try* to scan the verse. Line 1 ends with the aforementioned sawed-off *trochee,* and line 3 is all over the place (*anapest-iamb-anapest,* then what, an *amphibrach?*) And line 4!! Try a *hypermetrical* to start, followed by a *trochee* and two *iambs;* OR try the line as an *iamb,* two *trochees,* and an *iamb;* OR, my **final** choice— consider an *iamb* plus two *anapests.* (Crazy, huh?) Sometimes, it's best just to stick with the *beats*, something everyone can inherently follow with their own two ears. That's why the audibly elastic *ballad* is not only a *folk song,* but also a form that displays itself in a unique context, one that is dear to all of us— even those who try hard to abhor poetry. Here's a basic *ballad* stanza everybody knows (forget FEET; count only BEATS):

MAry HAD a LITtle LAMB	4 beats
its FLEECE was WHITE as SNOW	3 beats
and EVeryWHERE that MAry WENT	4 beats
the LAMB was SURE to GO.	3 beats

Can't get simpler than that. Yep, *nursery rhymes* are part of the genre, and the legendary Mother Goose (Ma Mère l'Oye, in France) was as much a poet, by vocation, as was John Milton. And we never forgot about Mary, did we. In fact, all these ballad approaches are primarily *accentual*— and perhaps that's why the ballad form is truly timeless. It's the inherently *musical* nature of the form, the audible voice of common people— one for all ages, without age.

Beyond songs and nursery rhymes, however, the ballad has been used to forward great poetic narratives for centuries. One the most famous is, for me, also one of the most consistently beautiful examples of the form— Samuel Taylor Coleridge's *The Rime of the Ancient Mariner.*

This excerpt likely rings in the ears:

> Water, water, every where,
> And all the boards did shrink;
> Water, water, every where,
> Nor any drop to drink.
>
> The very deep did rot: O Christ!
> That ever this should be!
> Yea, slimy things did crawl with legs
> Upon the slimy sea.
>
> About, about, in reel and rout
> The death-fires danced at night;
> The water, like a witch's oils,
> Burnt green, and blue and white.

And here's a profound snippet from Oscar Wilde's "The Ballad of Reading Gaol":

> And all men kill the thing they love,
> By all let this be heard
> Some do it with a bitter look,
> Some with a flattering word,
> The coward does it with a kiss,
> The brave man with a sword!

Note that in Wilde's poem, the ballad stanza contains six lines instead of four. Many of Coleridge's stanzas also employ six lines.

The fact that the ballad form is so simple-seeming leads newcomers to it early. Its tension / release works well for story-based, narrative poetry, and often poets start writing in exactly that manner, since the ballad parallels the sort of event sequence and exposition they are used to in prose. For such widespread application, ballad form appears as a shiny rental car with the motor running. Since cars are prone to crash occasionally, the new poet should apprentice his driving skills in increments, and work toward making his or her ballads ring with some discernible truth— to transcend the natural ease and sweet lilt of the form against the ear, and say something really special.

You may find as you proceed that your message, what you really want to say, is too much for this very basic form. And that may be a sign you are growing as poet. Look, we are not Samuel Coleridge, Robert Burns, or Emily Dickinson. For that matter, we aren't, guitars in hand, Woody Guthrie or Bob Dylan. But it doesn't preclude us from aspiring to the venerable cadences of 4-3, 4-3. Great poems have been written in this form for hundreds of years. They are often made, however, by poets who have mastered more elaborate-seeming, yet *more forgiving* forms, too. If you like, start here; see where it goes. Unlike the lamb, you follow Mary only if she's going where you are.

FORMS: PART FIVE— THE SESTINA

There are those who write sestinas just to show how godawfully smart they are. And indeed, writing poems whose lines repeat last words in a bizarre, extended pattern over six, six-line stanzas (plus a short, specialized 3-line "tag" stanza) does take cleverness. However, so does threading a needle blindfolded, or getting backstage at a rock concert. Neither of those pursuits, however, require much artistic sensibility. So, for our purposes, let's avoid the neat tricks, and go for something more. **Repetition**, whether dictated in a villanelle, pantoum (covered later), or otherwise judiciously used for its incessant impact, as in Tennyson's "Break, Break, Break," can carry a poem, and wholly justify the form in which it appears. But the key to success rests with *how* the device is used, and the content it supports. In the sestina, that "how" should be the entire reason to attempt one. Often, too often, it isn't.

In discussing sestinas and other, even more exotic forms, one can easily confuse real poetry with purely artisan-type craft, comparing say, needlepoint on potholders to Monet's "Water Lilies," or facades of your local mall to the Taj Mahal. We see among too many poets, artifice without art, craft as pattern— no voice, no music. But if the poet is truly *inspired,* truly has something to say, *then* his craft can enhance the message. Remember— *content* trumps form! For instance, Ezra Pound wrote some challenging pieces, even if, by way of *forms,* he wasn't a sestina specialist (with thanks). He did however, write one of the most famous sestinas extant, called "Sestina: Alaforte." Here's the first two stanzas, in the basic sestina form. Note that this sestina follows a nominal pattern of accentual pentameter. (Sestinas usually have a uniform meter of some kind throughout, although, given the constant shuffling of embroidered lines, that's not a requirement.)

Damn it all! all this our South stinks peace.
You whoreson dog, Papiols, come! Let's to music!
I have no life save when the swords clash.
But ah! When I see the standards gold, vair, purple,
        opposing,
And the broad fields beneath them turn crimson,
Then howls my heart nigh mad with rejoicing.

In hot summer have I great rejoicing
When the tempests kill the earth's foul peace,
And the lightnings from black heav'n flash crimson,
And the fierce thunders roar me their music
And the winds shriek through the clouds mad, opposing,
And through all the riven skies God's swords clash.

In the excerpt above, the repetition of words does not seem planned, yet it is. And the reinforcement of the words that are repeated, though separated in their placement— hammers the reader with harsh urgency in the pounding (and soon, jumbled) repetitions that battle holds. As wild as these lines are (you should hear him READ them), the sestina form works here. What *is* that form?

Examine the end-words of each line in the first stanza— (in order):
A. peace, B. music, C. clash, D. opposing, E. crimson, F. rejoicing.

Now check the planned end-words of each line in the second stanza:
F. rejoicing, A. peace, E., crimson, B. music, D. opposing, C. clash.
Yes, there IS a pattern to all this— and it plays out through the other stanzas in its own complicated way. The full scheme of repeated

end-words, including the first two stanzas and on through to that last regular stanza (followed by a tag stanza we'll also describe) is this way: **ABCDEF, FAEBDC, CFDABE, ECBFAD, DEACFB, BDFECA.** Beyond the last of six regular, six-line stanzas, there is a three-line tag, a mini-stanza if you like, called an **envoy.** The envoy's lines end with **ECA** or **ACE,** although **B, D,** or **F** may occur inside the lines.

Pound ended his sestina with:

> And let the music of the swords make them crimson!
> Hell grant soon we hear again the swords clash!
> Hell blot black for always the thought "Peace!"

Pound's positioning of graphic words and concepts in his end-lines, interrelated in changing meaning throughout, carries the day. Was this easy to accomplish? NO. Most of the time, poets are content to even *complete* a sestina form; to expect real content as well is a tall order. Objectively, you follow the scheme. *Subjectively,* you attempt to move the reader around as words weigh, and thoughts shift. This is why, as with the sonnet and the villanelle we have covered previously, there is (or should be) a palpable change in tone as the poem progresses to its end, with repeated words and phrases altering their angles for effect.

Some years ago I decided to take up the form in a self-challenging way— basing a sestina on a psalm from the Bible. I chose at random the 60th, certainly not the most distinguished from a literary point of view (spiritual content notwithstanding), yet in terms of creating lines from a select batch of end-words, as good as any. Remember, the point is to go beyond the form— to use form only to frame and help reveal actual *content.* Here's the full poem.

SESTINA FOR THE SIXTIETH PSALM

And my legions fall, prostrate or scattered
in the distant mist, lines turned to breaches
nulled in reach from the far face of holiness
and sickened to a man, the right, the left hand
waving to surrender before our pledged city?
Wanting, wallowed at progress of their armies,
the cold, clank regimenting of their armies
disciplined in death and refusing to be scattered
in the ply of patience that takes a city—
darkly marshaled foot-falls find our breaches,
shed resolve, cuff the even hand,
aspire to defy the bond of holiness
and by such crimes belie that holiness,
ring in the hollow of unwilling armies
raised to prop or splint the shaking hand
yet render self as fodder to be scattered
like a fist of rye in windy breaches—
seeds that fall on stone in an empty city.
Wine-astonished vision! blur the city
to the hallow of your word, your holiness
to turn two allies tight to four in breaches
and to lines affront these foreign-facing armies
unto salt of Edom's valley; scattered
as a flame with iron-casting hand
(to burn the dead denials with that hand!)—
your wake, the smoking stubble of their city,
right reversing, rigor black and scattered
at the rally of the hours of our holiness,
their gray and green disintegrated armies

offer mortared walls that mark their breaches
to testament, to the apex of their breaches,
offering sequestered peace with open hand
and glint of word translating arms and armies
into hilted swords, salvation of a city
and city yet recalled, within your holiness—
its own stone heart, its landbound pride, scattered
to the banners flown, to shepherd scattered
armies in your hand and heal in balm of holiness
the breaches of belief of man, and city.

Now, it doesn't sound half-bad when read aloud, but I've never been really happy with the poem— nor was I emboldened as I had originally projected, to take on *all* the psalms in this manner. Had I done so years ago, I would certainly be working on that project *still,* and who knows, perhaps on this same poem!

We've made our case; sestinas sap one's labor. But should you want to try one, go ahead. Like a medieval master, you must work a tapestry that ennobles its form, and move from artisan to artist. That panel, heavy, intricate, must display not only a remarkable surface, but also an underpinning of integrity and real worth. There is *so much* form in the sestina; without your planning and sweat, we expect the tapestry AND its wall could fall in on you quickly. So be advised. Meanwhile, we'll order up dogs and heavy equipment to sniff and dig you out.

FORMS: PART SIX— HAIKU: BEYOND THE 5-7-5

The venerable form of **haiku** starts more poets on their way than any other. Unfortunately, that way is not always the right way, and does not often enough make good poets. Further, it even less often makes good haikuists. Why? The poet mistakes the simplistic for the simple, and formula for substance. Is haiku easy to understand? On the surface, yes. But only on the surface. **Haiku** is an objective, *Japanese* short poem (usually untitled) based on a nature theme, with three lines consisting of the following number of syllables per line: five, then seven, then five. Note the stress of the word "Japanese"— because this poem is definitely grounded in an Eastern culture whose language and intent is far removed from our Western tongues and even, Western minds. With such change, comes expansion of the definition.

In Japanese poetic tradition, haiku is actually a relative newcomer. What has been known in the West as haiku are the first three lines ("opening part") culled from classic **renga** or from the five-line **tanka** of **haikai renga**, with a rule added that these short poems be nature based, containing a *kigo,* or "season word"— a flower, a bird, a fruit, snow, thunder, etc. The delivery of these poems is matter-of-fact— objective to a point where simplicity and clarity become transcendent. Frequently, haiku has been identified as a complement or medium for the practice of Zen Buddhism. By evoking the simple, one looks for the universal.

One should not confuse haiku with **senryu,** another three-line, 5-7-5 style that is NOT nature-based, and is much more open in both subject matter (including the human side of existence) and subjective viewpoint, incorporating at times, even humor and political content.

And here, right here, is where new poets go wrong. Haiku and senyru are not easy to write. With these forms, you are creating a snapshot of nature, or of life, and the shutter speed is FAST. Every word not only counts, every word carries the weight of 12 million pounds, yet combines to a paradox that carries *no weight at all.*

The one vital demand of the nature-based haiku and its human-based cousin, senryu, is that you must think *whole poem,* not line by line. If you think by line, you will tend to produce short telegrams of drivel. (In fact, all poets should be thinking whole poem with *every* kind of piece they write— but haiku's inherent brevity forces you to do that, if you're serious about writing anything approaching a good example of the form.)

A concept must be there first; then, you return to it, having already mined the diamond, to polish off any imperfection. And here's that promised expansion of the basic haiku definition: the imperfection to which I alluded has *nothing* to do with the syllables— nothing to do with— I see you counting on fingers or clicking off castanets— that blasted 5-7-5.

I don't care if you write your haiku or senryu in strict 5-7-5— ***and this is not blasphemy.*** True, classic Japanese haiku and senryu *are* in 5-7-5— IN JAPANESE. Japanese syllables, however, do not resemble English syllables *in any way.* Therefore, if you hold to *English* 5-7-5, to the point where you must eliminate the exact word that completes what spiritual and aesthetic concept your haiku demands— then you have committed, to my thinking, the ultimate blasphemy. Forget this heavy stress on 5-7-5. If your haiku is 5-7-5, fine; if it's not, fine too.

Consider the most famous haiku ever written in English, by Ezra Pound:

IN A STATION OF THE METRO

The apparition of these faces in the crowd;
Petals on a wet, black bough.

Ladies and gentlemen: that IS haiku. *But what about 5-7-5?* Forget it. What about the two lines instead of three? And a *title?* For purists out there, haiku went through more than a century where the three lines were incorporated into just one. (Many Japanese-written tanka[s] have also abandoned their own five-line structure.) So please, look beyond a static form— master form only to find essence. If you do, you have claim to the art. If you don't, and this is in English, not Japanese, we have a day job waiting for you at the Department of Stultified Poetics. Confused? In addition to the above example, try reading actual translations of classic Japanese haiku and senryu that carry their true poetic spirit into English. A collection by Robert Hass, America's past Library of Congress Laureate, would be a good start. (Note how many poems are *not* 5-7-5, certainly not in English. Or, if you're in a "subterranean" mood, listen to Beat poet Jack Kerouac reading from his freewheeling American haiku collection, *Mexico City Blues* (with jazz saxophone accompaniment, no less).

In other words, come up from the simplistic form to the *truly simple*, meaning the *essential,* and learn the concept of whole poem by moving away from just counting the syllables in a line. If you can do that, like those many faithful artists out there who devote their lives to haiku and other Japanese-based poetry, you will create beautiful, essential, and profound art, and be able to move easily and well into various forms of Western poetry, too. If you don't, you will just keep on writing these redundant, sort-of-placid-looking 5-7-5 things until they bore you and everybody else to death. Don't do that.

Because you will not, not really, be writing haiku.

FORMS: PART SEVEN— FROM COMMON PUDDINGS, TO THE HONEYPOT OF EXOTICA

If you like to experiment or work with common or exotic fixed forms, you'll find all you need in the *Princeton Encyclopedia of Poetry and Poetics* (ed. Preminger, A., Brogan, T. V. F., Fine Communications). Many of these forms perplex the uninitiated with their rhyme schemes, line make-ups, and hidden meanings.

Saving the vital chapters on **blank verse** and **free verse** for the last of our "forms" forays, here is a rather concise list of items (both verse forms and full poem forms) that we've not yet covered, from a sweet and wily panoply created across many lands over literally thousands of years.

IMPORTANT NOTES, REPEATED:
*In describing the rhyme scheme of a poem, each new and **different** end-rhyme, along with rhyming mates that follow in later lines, will share the **same letter** in the scheme's coded pattern, going through the alphabet **(a, b, c...)** in sequence, with unrhymed lines marked **x**. For instance, an example of the form atop the next page **(acrostic—** although rhyme isn't actually required for that particular form) is carrying a rhyme scheme of **aabbccddd.***

*Repeated lines in any poem (as in the **villanelle** described earlier, or in the **pantoum, triolet, rondeau, etc.,** to follow) are denoted by CAPITALIZING the letters involved.*

ACROSTIC

Any poem whose lines' first letters vertically form either the alphabet, the poet's or dedicatee's name, a concept word (which can look hokey, but not always), or even entire sentences, if the poem is long. Rhyme (or not), line length, and cadence are up the poet. This general form goes back to the Babylonians, but many poets, even modern ones, have fooled around with them. (Anne Sexton did, for instance.)

Here's a famous example from Edgar Allan Poe:

> **E**lizabeth it is in vain you say
> "**L**ove not"— thou sayest it in so sweet a way:
> **I**n vain those words from thee or L.E.L.
> **Z**antippe's talents had enforced so well:
> **A**h! if that language from thy heart arise,
> **B**reathe it less gently forth— and veil thine eyes.
> **E**ndymion, recollect, when Luna tried
> **T**o cure his love— was cured of all beside—
> **H**is folly— pride— and passion— for he died.

PANTOUM (from Pantun)

This poem started in Malaya centuries ago as a kind of proverb made of a single, four-line stanza (quatrain), where the first couplet states a direct notion, and the second, an altered look at the same subject, a "punch line couplet," often coming out of nowhere:

Doubtful fears that God is dead
and that's why men are meaner;
hopeful says that God's alive,
living in Argentina.

Yes, "meaner" is a goofy word, goofier still when you're rhyming it with "Argentina"— but I think I wrote that rhyme in the sixth grade, and it serves the purpose here as a rough example of a "proverbial" quatrain. That one was rhymed **xbxb.** In the classic **pantun,** the rhyme scheme would be **abab**, and sometimes those old poems actually went on for 6-12 lines rather than a standard 4, building upon their wise pronouncements as they went. Soon, pantun style appeared among the literary spices that had somehow traded their way to Europe.

Made popular in the nineteenth century, the French and English call their more elaborate form the **pantoum,** a poem in which the *second* and *fourth* lines of a stanza become the first and third lines of the next stanza, and lace together like a corset as the poem of proceeds. The modern pantoum can be any length the poet wishes. It will usually end (at least the English version does) with the first line of the poem repeated as the last line of the poem, and the third line of the poem (third line of the first quatrain) as the second line of the last quatrain. Got that?

Let's review. Diagramming the entire, ongoing repetition pattern, the lines would run **ABAB BCBC CDCD, etc**., until the ending stanza is reached. That **ending stanza,** upon arrival, repeats the second and fourth lines of the previous stanza as its first and third lines. It also repeats the third line of the *first* stanza, as its (the ending stanza's) second line, and the first line of the *first* stanza as the ending stanza's fourth line. So the poem ends as it began. You *sure* you got that?

Despite the silly musing in that old-style *pantun*, the pantoum need not be humorous. Rather, a pantoum could be purposefully wise (remember the old "proverbial" style), and build with touches of irony, using those striking line repetitions as it proceeds (combined with altered meaning we also saw in the sonnet, villanelle, and sestina), and climbing to a "big finish," or to some more gentle, yet still incisive conceit.

Here's a very well-crafted pantoum from a favorite colleague, Diana Weiss. Note that a pantoum can be in a regular meter or, as shown, in a freer pattern of feet or accents, so long as the repetitive-line form is followed. Rhyme might appear, but in a pantoum, it's not necessary.

NIGHT OF THE LITTLE GODS

Harmonious, flutes entwine
within adobe walls.
Shadows cast to call the spirit
of wandering Kokopelli.

Within adobe walls
voices rise in song
of wandering Kokopelli.
Couples sway, entranced and warmed,

voices rise in song.
Readying themselves,
couples sway, entranced and warmed;
anticipate the mating yet to come.

Readying themselves,
recalling promise of fertility,
anticipate the mating yet to come,
reach out ancestral hands.

Recalling promise of fertility,
shadows cast to call the spirit,
reach out ancestral hands. . .
Harmonious, flutes entwine.

LIMERICK

As you'll recall in our discussion on multi-syllable or "feminine" rhyme and its inherent sweet or humorous sound in poems, I referred derisively to the limerick as a vehicle for bawdy banter in bars. Well, it has always been that, and still is. But this generally funny Irish poetic form has endeared itself to many as part of "the people's poetry," useful BECAUSE of its humorous lilt and lighthearted content. So be it. Famous poets such as Edward Lear and Ogden Nash have specialized in well-crafted, humorous poetry, and have done the form justice— slave though it is to its magnficent lilt, and the predictable laughter that trails it.

The form: it's short— 5 lines. The first two lines have three feet, the next two lines have two feet, the last line, back to three feet. The feet employed throughout the poem are usually **anapests** (da da DUH) or **amphibrachs** (da DUH da). Each produce a nice, easy canter. You *can* use other types of feet, too; yet that special pair of rhythms, as if trained into horses happy in their paces, carry most limericks.

Line 3 and line 4 sometimes will jettison their first anapests for iambs; others will disregard the presence of unaccented end-syllables. But like the use of spices or garlic in a broth, such recipes can be followed "to taste." The rhyme scheme is **aabba.**

It is the combination of multi-syllable words, and especially the multi-syllable, feminine *end-rhymes,* as well as the lilting rhythm of the anapest itself that makes the poem sound so light, so easily funny, almost without regard to what the words actually *mean.* When you incorporate sound devices like alliteration, assonance, consonance, or *onomatopoeia* (words that sound like the natural effects they emulate), combined with obviously humorous ideas— little wonder this form has become synonymous with poetic comedy.

An example:

> There is not for a man enough sense
> in the present or futures of tense
> to resist that ensnare
> on the sirensong stair
> where a woman awaits, and relents.

That one was mine, uniformly anapestic.

Here's Edward Lear. It's fully anapestic, too, save for the one almost unnoticeable, and allowable, extra syllable at the very end.

> There was an Old Person of Harrow
> Who bought a mahogany barrow,
> For he said to his wife
> "You're the joy of my life!
> And I'll wheel you all day in this barrow!"

Limericks were originally crafted to be *obscene,* and it remained so for a long time, but this is no longer the case. Names of person and place usually reside in the first line, though the poem's focus could involve some concept or object. Notice also an old convention, that of repeating a subject from a previous line, often the first line, but in Lear's poem above, it's the second. Such repetitions, however, are not required. In fact, keeping with its lightheartedness, the form doesn't command *any* particular orthodoxy. A closer look will spot a shaved-off syllable in line 1 of the Rudyard Kipling limerick below:

> There was a small boy of Quebec
> Who was buried in snow to his neck
> When they said "Are you friz?"
> He replied, "Yes, I is—
> But we don't call this cold in Quebec."

Whatever you decide, uniformity to your own particular concept of the limerick, and both good subject matter and rhymes, are the keys.

TERZA RIMA

A verse form which can be used in a poem of any length. The 14th century master, Dante (Alighieri) set his *Divine Comedy* in terza rima. The form consists of three-line stanzas (tercets) whose lines rhyme in an interlocking pattern: **aba, bcb, cdc, ded,** etc. Poems written in this style, as well as individual sections in longer poems, end with *either* a single line or a couplet (two lines) that rhymes with the middle line of the last tercet.

Example, from Shelley's "Ode to the West Wind," Section I:

> O wild West Wind, thou breath of Autumn's being,
> Thou, from whose unseen presence the leaves dead
> Are driven, like ghosts from an enchanter fleeing,
>
> Yellow, and black, and pale, and hectic red,
> Pestilence-stricken multitudes: O thou,
> Who chariotest to their dark wintry bed
>
> The wingèd seeds, where they lie cold and low,
> Each like a corpse within its grave, until
> Thine azure sister of the Spring shall blow
>
> Her clarion o'er the dreaming earth, and fill
> (Driving sweet buds like flocks to feed in air)
> With living hues and odours plain and hill:
>
> Wild Spirit, which art moving everywhere;
> Destroyer and Preserver; hear, O hear!

And each section that follows in the poem starts its own, new terza rima pattern. (Note that an **ode,** like Shelley's, is a lyric poem that evokes deep thought or feeling, and is often used to celebrate some person, place, thing, or idea; terza rima lines seem perfect for that.) Besides Dante and Shelley, terza rima poets include Chaucer, Wyatt, and Auden; count Derek Walcott, too, in his modern epic, *Omeros.*

OTTAVA RIMA

Also from the medieval Italian, it's a stanza form consisting of 8 lines, each originally 11 syllables, which was then shortened in English to 10 syllables, in iambic pentameter. (Note, however, that the evolution of accentual-syllabic meter, especially in English, has de-emphasized or eliminated the form's syllable count.) The rhyme scheme is **abababcc.** Ottava rima has been employed many times in long poems of its original period and since, lending itself especially to romantic and later, heroic narratives. The form has served Spenser, Shelley, and Browning. Lord Byron used ottava rima in several major poems, the most famous being his masterpiece, *Don Juan.*

An excerpt:

> There is an awkward thing which much perplexes,
> Unless like wise Tiresias we had proved
> By turns the difference of the several sexes;
> Neither can show quite *how* they would be loved.
> The sensual for a short time but connects us,
> The sentimental boasts to be unmoved;
> But both together form a kind of centaur,
> Upon whose back 'tis better not to venture.

CANZONE

From the Italian, again from Dante's and Petrarch's time, the **canzone** is one of the song-forms that would become a stand-alone poetic structure of common use; it was an early contemporary of the sonnet. The verse form is in iambic pentameter (the original had lines of 11 syllables, and a consistent number of lines— anywhere from 7 to 20— within each stanza). There were five or six stanzas, concluding with an additional, shorter envoy-stanza. Also, the last line of each stanza usually rhymed with the first line of the succeeding stanza.

The canzone was adapted into English in the sixteenth century by Scottish poet William Drummond of Hawthornden, and the form underwent various changes and experiments, some of which were incorporated into the work of Spenser and Milton.

What follows is an example of the form (note the host of changes from the original description) by John Milton. Milton, in fact, wrote this canzone in Italian, and it was later translated into English by William Cowper:

CANZONE

They mock my toil— the nymphs and am'rous swains—
And whence this fond attempt to write, they cry,
Love-songs in language that thou little know'st?
How dar'st thou risque to sing these foreign strains?
Say truly. Find'st not oft thy purpose cross'd,
And that thy fairest flow'rs, Here, fade and die?
Then with pretense of admiration high—
Thee other shores expect, and other tides,

Rivers on whose grassy sides
Her deathless laurel-leaf with which to bind
Thy flowing locks, already Fame provides;
Why then this burthen, better far declin'd?
    Speak, Muse! For me— The Fair One said who guides
My willing heart, and all my Fancy's flights,
"This is the language in which Love delights."

The songlike nature of the canzone was always more important than its rote form. In English, canzones became more flexible as to number of stanzas, use of rhyme among the lines, syllable count (if counted at all), actual size and division of stanzas, and use of envoys. That flexibility makes it useful for today's poets who may want to go farther afield in fixed forms than the sonnet. They can enjoy a degree of freedom in sculpting particular poetic ideas, yet remain within the general discipline of a form they can, for that poem, ultimately invent.

A more disciplined style of canzone includes repeated end-words, as in a sestina. W. H. Auden worked the form into a rather elaborate stew. His "Canzone" has five stanzas and an envoy or coda. Each stanza has twelve lines, the coda, six, and cycles the end words (even in the coda) according to a unique recipe. Often poets, especially famous ones, will become noted for their take on a specific verse form or whole form, championing one particular style or inventing a new one, and others will copy the approach. Ultimately, this expansive form— whether in length, line characteristics, rhyme (if any), etc., becomes exactly what YOU want it to be. So long as you are consistent with your plan throughout, you will, as was broadly shown in the previous paragraphs, still be writing a canzone.

TRIOLET

The triolet has one stanza, eight lines. The lines are iambic tetrameter (four feet per line). The first, fourth and seventh lines are identical. The second and last lines, also identical. As a result, the poem's initial couplet is the same as the final couplet. Scheme is **ABaAabAB**. (A *small letter* identifies lines with a specific **end-rhyme**. If a whole line is **repeated**, that line will always be identified by a *capital* letter.) An example, "How Great My Grief," from Thomas Hardy:

> How great my grief, my joys how few,
> Since first it was my fate to know thee!
> — Have the slow years not brought to view
> How great my grief, my joys how few,
> Nor memory shaped old times anew,
>   Nor loving-kindness helped to show thee
> How great my grief, my joys how few,
>   Since first it was my fate to know thee?

As with villanelles or sestinas, the repetition you hear in the lines should fall naturally on the ear within the context of the poem's progress, and as it moves along, though repeated, those words and phrases, subtly or viscerally, change in meaning.

CINQUAIN

A form borrowed from the Japanese (although there are other five-line poems bearing some similarity that came out of Europe), and it has many variants today. One basic style dictates content, each line building the description (expanding the meaning) of the subject in line 1.

Line 1: one word (subject, a noun)

Line 2: two words (adjectives)

Line 3: three words (action verbs)

Line 4: four words (feelings, in the form of a phrase)

Line 5: one word (synonym of the word in line 1, relating a subtle change perhaps, or summation)

If that sounds potentially simplistic rather than merely *simple* (the rite of haiku) it can be written too easily as such. Students are sometimes taught these as their "hello" to poetry; they are "blind dates" that usually don't end well, nipping prospective acolytes right out of the seed. Of course, with some would-be poets—those who can't escape the surface fluff of forms like this— we pray that it *had.*

Additional demands on the cinquain have to do with syllabic meter based on syllable count per line, or as total count within the poem.

The popular American form of the cinquain was developed by poet Adelaide Crapsey, as a variation of her study of the Japanese **tanka**. She took this work seriously, and so ubiquitous has this specific form become that it is known as the **Crapsey Cinquain**.

Crapsey's syllable-counts for the five lines are: 2 / 4 / 6 / 8 / 2.

You will also find, if you look, attention to establishing a set number of *stresses* in each line, so that syllable groups are audibly enhanced. The addition etches a recognizable pattern beneath the line sequence containing the following numbers of "beats": 1, 2, 3, 4, and 1 again. While that planning has been ignored by some scholars, I agree with those who say the stresses may be as important as the syllable count. In any event, there are many other specific varieties of this *general* form, as listed below:

reverse cinquain: five-line syllabic verse of the pattern 2 / 8 / 6 / 4 / 2
mirror cinquain: a sequence of standard cinquains followed by a reverse cinquain
butterfly cinquain: nine-line syllabic verse of the pattern 2 / 4 / 6 / 8 / 2 / 8 / 6 / 4 / 2
crown cinquain: a sequence of five cinquains
garland cinquain: a sequence of six cinquains in which the final cinquain is composed of lines from the preceding five (generally Line 1 from Stanza 1, Line 2 from Stanza 2, Line 3 from Stanza 3 and so on).

Is all this worth the trouble? On her version, Crapsey certainly thought so, and she really did work this form successfully, with content and style as well as "form."

BALLADE
Not to be confused with the English *ballad*, a form that we have already covered— the **ballade** made the reputation of the poet-troubadour Francois Villon more than six centuries ago. The Bob Dylan of his time, Villon employed a crafty, complex method that like today's popular song, went well with musical accompaniment. Also, as with the folk or pop song, the ballade employs a repeated line, or **refrain.** There are several variants, but here's the basic formula:

3 stanzas, 8 lines apiece (**octave**s), followed by
1 stanza of 4 lines, the **envoy** (a **quatrain**).

One line is repeated as a **refrain** at the end of each stanza, including the envoy. There are 8 syllables per line throughout. Rhyme scheme for each octave is **ababbcbC.** Rhyme scheme for the envoy is **cbC.** (The refrain, **C,** steers the poem, so it *must* be a strong line.)

A longer variant is called **ballade supreme;** in this style, the eight-line stanzas go to **ten** lines each, the four-line envoy goes to **five** lines, and the syllable count in each line of the poem goes from eight to **ten.** The rhyme scheme in all the ten-line stanzas becomes **ababbcbcD** and in the five-line envoy, becomes **ccdcD.**

Either of these ballade types are modified further by *doubling* them to *six* stanzas before the envoy, instead the usual three. Simple? **No.** Elaborations of form over decades, or centuries, will create **a)** change for change's sake; and **b)** new avenues of genius. Take your pick here.

RONDEAU
An old French form originally devised to work in tandem with musical accompaniment (and directly synonymous with the *rondo,* its true musical counterpart), yet passed down to us as a stand-alone poetic construction. It contains 15 lines based on two sets of rhymes. There are three stanzas— five lines, then four lines, then six lines. Generally, there are breaks between each stanza, but modern versions often eschew them. The rhyme scheme is: first stanza **aabba;** second stanza **aab** plus a repeated refrain-line **C;** third stanza **aabba** with concluding refrain **C.** The refrain is typically the *first phrase* stated in the first line that keys the subject matter of the poem, and that may change in emphasis, tone, or even meaning by poem's end. Just as in the villanelle and some other forms, one expects the refrain to carry

the poem along, and that the line itself will increase in impact, or alter in meaning or tone upon its repeating.

Example, John McCrae:

IN FLANDERS FIELDS

In Flanders fields the poppies blow
Between the crosses, row on row
That mark our place; and in the sky
The larks, still bravely singing, fly
Scarce heard amid the guns below.

We are the Dead. Short days ago
We lived, felt dawn, saw sunset glow,
Loved and were loved, and now we lie
In Flanders fields.

Take up our quarrel with the foe:
To you from failing hands we throw
The torch; be yours to hold it high.
If ye break faith with us who die
We shall not sleep, though poppies grow
In Flanders fields.

A variation on the rondeau is the English **roundel**, which reduces the line count from 13 to 11. The first and last stanzas have four lines (quatrains) and the middle stanza has three (tercet). The first and third stanzas end with a repeated line (refrain) from the first part of the poem's first line. There is a space-break between each of the stanzas. Rhyme scheme is **abaC bab abaC,** with **C** as the refrain.

A heart-rending example from its originator, Charles Algernon Swinburne:

A BABY'S DEATH (excerpt)

The little eyes that never knew
Light other than of dawning skies,
What new life now lights up anew
The little eyes?

Who knows but on their sleep may rise
Such light as never heaven let through
To lighten earth from Paradise?
No storm, we know, may change the blue
Soft heaven that haply death descries
No tears, like these in ours, bedew
The little eyes.

A more elaborate form of the rondeau is the **rondeau redoublé**. It has five stanzas of four lines each. Like the basic rondeau, it also has two rhymes, but more repetition of lines. The four lines of the first stanza become, in sequence, the *fourth* lines of stanzas 2 to 5, and the beginning of the first line is repeated as a shorter fifth line to conclude to sixth and final stanza. For a modern take on this form, try "Rondeau Redoublé (and Scarcely Worth the Trouble, at That)" by Dorothy Parker.

CLERIHEW

Another turn-of-century (19th to 20th) form named for its inventor— in this case, Edmund Clerihew Bentley. The form is reserved for personal, meaning biographical, sketches. The clerihew has four lines of irregular length (intended for comic effect), with the third and fourth typically longer than the others. The first line simply consists of the person's name. The tone is generally whimsical, as opposed to harsh; yet one could imagine satirical poets, the Swifts or Drydens among us, decking these things out in a resplendence of barbed wire.

The rhyme scheme is **aabb.** As with limericks, elongated, tortured rhymes are prized. In this way, the model really reminds me of those creative, daft inscriptions carved on odd headstones, after Irish wakes or New Orleans funerals. Mr. Bentley's very first *clerihew,* at age 16, is innocent enough:

> Sir Humphry Davy
> Was not fond of gravy.
> He lived in the odium
> Of having discovered sodium.

RHYME ROYAL

A verse form consisting of seven lines, usually in iambic pentameter, introduced in English in the fourteenth century by Geoffrey Chaucer. The rhyme scheme is **ababbcc.** The stanza groupings consist of one three-line stanza (tercet) and two couplets, with a rhyme scheme of **aba bb cc**, or a quatrain (four lines) and a tercet (three lines) with a rhyme scheme of **abab bcc**. The form has been used for many long narrative poems, but embellishes thoughtful, *lyric poems* as well.

Here's a famous example of the latter, from Thomas Wyatt:

THEY FLEE FROM ME

They flee from me, that sometime did me seek,
With naked foot stalking within my chamber.
Once have I seen them gentle, tame, and meek,
That now are wild, and do not once remember,
That sometime they have put themselves in danger
To take bread at my hand; and now they range
Busily seeking in continual change.
Thanked be Fortune, it hath been otherwise
Twenty times better; but once especial,
In thin array, after a pleasant guise,
When her loose gown did from her shoulders fall,
And she me caught in her arms long and small,
And therewithal sweetly did me kiss,
And softly said, "Dear heart, how like you this?"
It was no dream; for I lay broad awaking:
But all is turn'd now through my gentleness,
Into a bitter fashion of forsaking;
And I have leave to go of her goodness;
And she also to use new fangleness.
But since that I unkindly so am served:
How like you this, what hath she now deserved?

FORMS: PART EIGHT— BLANK VERSE—
THE BLOODSTREAM OF MASTERPIECES

Well, we waited until near the end of our "forms" discussion to address **blank verse**. That befits the preeminent status it maintains as a verse form— the life-giving circulatory system of its body, rather than a body itself. Blank verse is essentially the *unrhymed* counterpart of many types of poems written in tetrameter, pentameter, hexameter, or whatever number of regular feet to the line. (It is usually iambic, but not rigidly so.) Imagine a sonnet, a villanelle, or any poetic form in a regular meter that is without planned end-rhymes. It can be whatever length you like. So long as the meter stays the same within its own context, you have blank verse.

But let me tell you something— you have more than that. Blank verse fills Shakespeare's plays; it arrests John Milton's *Paradise Lost*. In this verse, you have Wordsworth, Shelley. You also have Browning, Frost, (Hart) Crane, Stevens. In sum, you have the core of our poetry in English, much of it the greatest ever written— and it awaits you.

At the start of their careers, poets spend too much time dancing with rhymed forms. They stumble because they have not first found the voice and measure of their own expression, before attempting to color poems with the artifice of rhyme. Read from works of any of the masters above. You'll find poetry of profound intellect, of exposition that matters beyond the cute effect of the last greeting card you opened. Here is where you will probably learn, better than anywhere else, to write really fine poetry, and what you learn you will then take in any direction— to other fixed forms, including rhymed forms, or to free verse. Or, intoxicated, you will just *stay there.*

This is Robert Browning— as he assumes the character of a semi-delusional, broken man, sending his likely unfaithful wife off to her "cousin" in the conclusion of the dramatic poem, "Andrea del Sarto":

> I am grown peaceful as old age to-night.
> I regret little, I would change still less.
> Since there my past life lies, why alter it?
> The very wrong to Francis!— it is true
> I took his coin, was tempted and complied,
> And built this house and sinned, and all is said.
> My father and my mother died of want.
> Well, had I riches of my own? you see
> How one gets rich! Let each one bear his lot.
> They were born poor, lived poor, and poor they died:
> And I have laboured somewhat in my time
> And not been paid profusely. Some good son
> Paint my two hundred pictures— let him try!
> No doubt, there's something strikes a balance. Yes,
> You loved me quite enough, it seems to-night.
> This must suffice me here. What would one have?
> In heaven, perhaps, new chances, one more chance—
> Four great walls in the New Jerusalem,
> Meted on each side by the angel's reed,
> For Leonard, Rafael, Agnolo and me
> To cover— the three first without a wife,
> While I have mine! So— still they overcome
> Because there's still Lucrezia— as I choose.

> Again the Cousin's whistle! Go, my Love.

If you're inclined toward free verse (and we invite new poets to try their wings in free expression early), *but* you are having trouble knowing what to keep and what to throw out— come back to blank verse— you'll learn that here. Without the crutch or commandant of rhyme, you must rely on what you really have to say. Sometimes you'll end your statement at the end of a line, sometimes you'll carry it over, and **enjamb**. With experience, you will learn to match the natural flow of speech with the flow of your lines.

Here's Tennyson, enjambment positively *overflowing,* from *Ulysses*:

> It little profits that an idle king,
> By this still hearth, among these barren crags,
> Match'd with an aged wife, I mete and dole
> Unequal laws unto a savage race,
> That hoard, and sleep, and feed, and know not me.
> I cannot rest from travel: I will drink
> Life to the lees: All times I have enjoy'd
> Greatly, have suffer'd greatly, both with those
> That loved me, and alone, on shore, and when
> Thro' scudding drifts the rainy Hyades
> Vext the dim sea: I am become a name;
> For always roaming with a hungry heart
> Much have I seen and known; cities of men
> And manners, climates, councils, governments,
> Myself not least, but honour'd of them all;
> And drunk delight of battle with my peers,
> Far on the ringing plains of windy Troy.

Now, blank verse can remain "unrhymed" (meaning no regular pattern of end-rhymes) and yet include all manner of internal sound devices including assonance, consonance, and repetition— and still be blank verse. In "The Second Coming," W. B. Yeats employs the repeated consonance of the hard letter "d," repeats a line-ending word, "hand," and even rhymes it, imperfectly, with "sands" inside the stanza:

> Turning and turning in the widening gyre
> The falcon cannot hear the falconer;
> Things fall apart; the centre cannot hold;
> Mere anarchy is loosed upon the world,
> The blood-dimmed tide is loosed, and everywhere
> The ceremony of innocence is drowned;
> The best lack all convictions, while the worst
> Are full of passionate intensity.
>
> Surely some revelation is at hand;
> Surely the Second Coming is at hand.
> The Second Coming! Hardly are those words out
> When a vast image out of Spiritus Mundi
> Troubles my sight: somewhere in sands of the desert
> A shape with lion body and the head of a man,
> A gaze blank and pitiless as the sun,
> Is moving its slow thighs, while all about it
> Reel shadows of the indignant desert birds.
> The darkness drops again; but now I know
> That twenty centuries of stony sleep
> Were vexed to nightmare by a rocking cradle,
> And what rough beast, its hour come round at last,
> Slouches towards Bethlehem to be born?

How about the *meter* of blank verse? It's definitely not cast in quick-drying concrete. Due to the fact that most English expression hovers around tetrameter, pentameter, and occasionally hexameter, you will find this particular verse form helpful in controlling your voice, while not obscuring it with the ironclad need to meet an end-rhyme.

Truly, blank verse presents the best chance at natural expression and ordered thinking a poet may ever find within the terra incognita of his art. It is a form that can reinforce great statements, whether emotional or philosophical, and tell great stories. Engage *King Lear* or *Hamlet,* and spot all the blank verse; if you're good, you'll even find some of it cleverly hemmed into several fragments of a speech or dialogue. Shakespeare invites a subtle, marvelous brand of discovery with this form, since is something you feel anyway while reading or listening to many of his plays, whether you realize it or not.

Practice the discipline of blank verse, reasonably master it, and see your poetry, whatever kind you choose, change forever— much for the better. And if you think you have something important, maybe even profound to say, come here first. Blank verse is blood flowing through healthy veins, always, back to the heart of things.

FORMS: PART NINE— FREE VERSE

One might consider the term "free verse" self-explanatory— i.e., verse that is FREE— no rules, anything goes. Well, yes and no. It's true that you, the poet, dictate style (yes, there is style and also *structure* in whatever you may invent) within any free verse poem. So "free" becomes a nebulous term. Free from *what?* OK, we know what— mandatory verse forms, line lengths, stress or syllable count, rhyme schemes, word or line repetitions, etc. And the content? It can be of course, whatever you like.

Well, what *do* you like? And what will your *reader* like to read? You see, "freedom FROM" becomes an awfully unruly dictator without an idea of what is, by your design, your own "freedom TO."

Yes, you *can* do anything. But will it make good poetry? If I run my hand along a keyboard, is it music, or just sound? If I take a handful of red paint and smear it on a canvas, is it a painting, or just a blotch of color? Obviously, what you want to communicate is vital— and so is how you do it. However "free," free verse may seem, it yet requires substance, direction, technique and an absolute desire to communicate something in a specific way if it is to be successful verse, the *free* part notwithstanding.

It's true that the majority of poetry you see in magazines today, as well as that written by today's poets— including me, is in free verse. Therefore, the subject deserves at least as much attention as we would give the most elaborate, rule-laden, and complex "fixed" form. While we have touched on free verse throughout the book, here we account for some coordinated aspects of that particular discipline.

THE USE OF SPACE

As we've mentioned earlier, space for the poet is an element whose value is nearly inestimable, just as it is for the musician (as distance between notes) or the painter (as distance of objects in perspective). In fixed forms, it becomes like deft paint-strokes on the canvas of a collective block of printed words, a means of taking breaths here and there, of isolating a thought, of visually marking a way. How it is used may be closely governed.

But in free verse, we find a different tack. Try out the notion that the "canvas" flips, and use of space magnifies itself, becoming not just a selective type of paint, but also the broad canvas itself, right to left, up and down, as the entirety of that page's white volume now holds the inked (painted) or "pixeled" symbols and images— the creative, maybe innovative, and often intuitive groupings of the poet's mind.

As jazz strains boundaries of its own musical form and is frequently improvised, creating a new alliance between space and sound, the same dynamic exists in free verse. Here, the bond is between space and the strophes on a printed page. (If you recall, we had stated that free verse borrows an ancient poetic term, specially aligned for our modern purpose as counterpart to a fixed form's "stanza"— that being the label, "strophe.") Between these strophes, seen as spare fragments or thick with words and lines, is the use of *space*— with you as traffic cop amid the crossing thoroughfares.

As in prose, most poets, including many free verse poets (me too), will start at the left margin justification, and venture out from there. We may, at any point indent for effect, but unless we want to free the lines entirely for specific aims, our home port remains due west.

Example:

COPSE OF BIRCHES

Leonardo, *Drawing*, 1498-1502

Come from and to
this copse of birches more real
than I, more tactile, deep
and dense than the wood I walked to
in the morning of an old life,
        than the indistinct trunks
of my certainties, this copse, these trees
and what may lay beyond them
ask me to imagine more
than the artist intended or the world provides,
and isn't that irony good, chopped fodder
for a holocaust, a natural fuel
for pagan blaze, for small crosses,
for wine under shade.

Yet many poems (including the epics of Walt Whitman, Ezra Pound, W. C. Williams, Charles Olson, and Allen Ginsberg), are *not* confined to the left edge of the page. Lines *may* start there— or start *anywhere*. I suppose the most important idea to remember here is— getting the reader to willingly follow wherever you go. Most readers (unless we mean the readers of Arabic, Hebrew, Farsi or the like) collect their scripted language left to right— hence the originating "safe" anchor of the left margin. But our experience in reading or visually absorbing other images and symbols (signs, paintings, film and video, etc.) shows a willingness to scan a broad field for data or aesthetic content. In the following poem, which involves the sinking of the ocean liner *Andrea Doria,* I literally wanted all the human voices, fragments of humanity, to float around. So I used the "sea" of the page.

DORIA

Go to your station.

       Surrender your inhibitions now.
       Seal your soul-seams with tape
       and say what you mean.

Fasten your vest, sir.

              I have never been comfortable.
              I am a lingerer, chattel.

              And as estimable as lire.

       Hold me, like this, like a baby.

Step forward. Forward please.

              I have always been drowning;
              the air to me was water
              and I was submerged.

Il dolce suono
mi colpi di sua voce!...Ah quella voce
m'è qui nel cor discesa!...

There are biscuits in the boats.

> And I loved you as I loved
> my mother who let me breathe

> you bastard.

> > Little Sal-lee Wa-ter.

Back— back. Let it go!

> Oh my God my pearls my pearls
> my pearls!
> Let it go baby! Let it go.

— and they have two boys
and they have two girls.

> Hail Mary full of grace, the Lord is with thee.
> Blessed art thou among women and blessed
> is the fruit of thy womb, Jesus.

I'll bet
during the Flood, the sea
was not salty like this.

It was more like tears.

Hail Mary full of Grace,
the Lord is with thee—

Alfin son tua, alfin sei mio,
A me ti dona un Dio...

I forgive you.
But I
do not forgive me. That's
my penance

that, and this
you see.

All right, that was one reason to use the whole page. But the reasons
to take a poetic line (or lines) out to the right, back to the left, break in
pieces, or drop down precipitously, are many. Such may include:

to speed up, slow down, or abruptly stop a poetic statement; use
of space in this regard would tend to outstrip in impact the standard
effects of punctuation, although punctuation can work in tandem
with it;

to isolate a flash image for surprise or even shock value; the eye darts to the image, and the image, so isolated, responds to the eye;

to create a sensation of suspension, of floating, or crashing, where words go beyond their semantic selves and become separate objects of movement, or displacement;

to emphasize or set aside one idea or statement in the form a word, phrase, sentence, or even a poetic "paragraph," from the general discourse, to elevate it, question it, or even alter its meaning in relation to other ideas or statements. Such special fragmentation can increase the "volume" of a phrase, so the mind's ear may hear that extra bit of intonation, or exhortation, just as if the poem were being read aloud, or better yet, fully orated, as in the dramatic monologue. Additional visual aspects could include playing with font or size of the lettering, breaking words up (E. E. Cummings-style), or adding other visual symbols, such as the Chinese pictograms in Pound's famous *Cantos*.

As previously mentioned, and seen in enough examples here, standard punctuation still plays an important part in free verse, as poetic statements (phrases, clauses, or sentences) move across, down, and around the page. One element you have seen me using all the time is the **long dash** (near-cousin to the less impacting, multiple-hyphen-looking *double-dash*). Emily Dickinson loved the long dash tool and brought it to prominence. It can and has been used with profit in *any* form of verse, fixed or not, such is its ability to lengthen a pause in a line just a bit more, and render emphasis to the phrase or line that follows it. But when employed in the open vistas of free verse, the long dash will enliven, control, or conduct a flow as no other punctuation mark can. And beyond its rhythmic attributes, there's something to the *physical* character of the long dash that adds a visual flair to the work as it rests on the page, like that indelible, beautiful ink-stroke on rice paper. Experiment with it, and see.

LINE LENGTH (OR DEPTH)

Cummings and Williams loved short lines, immersing their brief statements in white space. Others, Whitman and Ginsberg especially, employ many long lines, pulling the reader who listens, albeit silently, to the very end of the poet's own breath in the completion of a dramatic conceit, and as if it were being delivered live, with passionate elocution.

From Walt Whitman's "Song of Myself":

> The smoke of my own breath,
> Echoes, ripples, buzz'd whispers, love-root silk thread,
>   crotch and vine,
> My respiration and inspiration, the beating of my heart,
>   the passing of blood and air through my lungs,
> The sniff of green leaves and dry leaves, and of the shore
>   and dark-color'd sea-rocks, and of hay in the barn,
> The sound of belch'd words of my voice loos'd
>   to the eddies of the wind,
> A few light kisses, a few embraces, a reaching around
>   of arms,
> The play of shine and shade on the trees as the supple
>   boughs wag,
> The delight alone or in the rush of the streets, or along
>   the fields and hill-sides,
> The feeling of health, the full-noon trill, the song of me
>   rising to meet the sun.

Actually, the typesetting of that excerpt is for our convenience, but depending on page size, the lines present sinuous persuasions, keyed to the fearless dynamics of the poet's voice. Commas, spaces, and occasional short lines provide visual "breath-cues," vital moments of almost physical pause, before Whitman launches rapturous anew.

A poet must think, however, not only in terms of line length, but also in the number of lines that may be set together as blocks or otherwise connected, whole islands of utterance, and calculate the effect such handiwork may cause. In this way, concern about the visual impact of lines goes beyond length, to the "depth" and sculpt of the print down the page. Within the fixed, accentual-syllabic verse of the past seven centuries, such line-by-line sculpt was predictable, even psychically comforting, a product of visual order and agreed-upon rhythm. From there, the method turned "law-and-leg-iron," enforced by academics and popular tradition. In *free verse,* regularity of lines is suspended, and minds, freed to make new ways, arrive at new vistas. Poets use bold strophe arrays, graphics, even shapes, as in the **concrete poem**— a modern *return* to Herbert's venerable "pattern poem." This work is at once a subject *and* a physical object, bonded to its page's canvas.

WHITHER METER?

Strict metering, rhyme schemes, and stanza forms that had dominated Western poetry were dashed in the credo of free verse. Revolt flashed not only in America but also in France, with the "vers libre" of Jules Laforgue (T. S. Eliot's early model), Arthur Rimbaud, and Stéphane Mallarmé. In their wake, a slow takeover commenced. The past, however, did not die; we still use fixed forms. Curiously, a casual check of Whitman finds cadences not entirely discarded in the fray. Instead, the poet moves in an idiom that carries any follower to the *King James*

Bible— to the ancient verse of the *Book of Psalms* and the *Song of Solomon.* Included here is the primeval legacy of bards and prophets, stringing stories aloud on the pins of gesture and emphasis— a purely *accentual* meter. (Playing on the idea of "past lives," we wonder if the writers of the *Bhagavad Gita* and *Ecclesiastes,* or if the persons, real or idealized, of Homer, Rumi, Villon, and Whitman, could all be one and the same.) Meanwhile, those French bomb-throwers of the late 19th century sought any vehicle that would free them from the rigid order of an unalterable, twelve-syllable, iambic-only *Alexandrine verse.* Rimbaud and company wanted to obliterate regular line lengths; in the process, they also blurred the line between poetry and prose.

Thus we discover the cousin of free verse, **the prose poem.** A prose poem is NOT a prose paragraph *called* a poem. Whether it contains the prose conventions of a paragraph, including punctuation, or not, there is in the prose poem a willful abandonment of sequential "story." If there is any story at all, it is immediate, a flash, and the language, as in other poetry, is heightened in its sonority, use of metaphor, and consciousness of the ebb and flow of cadence.

Many modern poets rejected the burgeoning form, doubting its worth as poetry; T. S. Eliot was among them. Still, it prospered beyond its French champions, appearing in Russia (Nikolai Gogol), in Poland (Boleslaw Prus), in Ireland (Oscar Wilde and James Joyce)— and finally in America, where it became a flexible resource for Ezra Pound, William Carlos Williams, and Allen Ginsberg.

One other famous exemplar was Amy Lowell. Of her slice-of-life takes on this form, one from 1916 called simply, "Bath," shimmers as many of these poems do, in the bright immediacy of present tense:

BATH

The day is fresh-washed and fair, and there is a smell of
tulips and narcissus in the air.

The sunshine pours in at the bath-room window and bores
through the water in the bath-tub in lathes and planes of
greenish-white. It cleaves the water into flaws like a jewel,
and cracks it to bright light.

Little spots of sunshine lie on the surface of the water and
dance, dance and their reflections wobble deliciously over
the ceiling; a stir of my finger sets them whirring, reeling.
I move a foot and the planes of light in the water jar.

I lie back and laugh, and let the green-white water, the sun-
flawed beryl water, flow over me. The day is almost too
bright to bear, the green water covers me from the too bright
day. I will lie here awhile and play with the water and the
sun spots. The sky is blue and high. A crow flaps by the window, and there is a whiff of tulips and narcissus in the air.

NARRATIVE, DRAMATIC, AND LYRIC POETRY

Poetry is divided into roughly three types— two closely aligned, one not as much. **Narrative poetry** involves a story. It could be news, it could be fantasy, but it's a story. The reader follows along. **Dramatic poetry** can be narrative too, only it focuses on dialogue, on extended monologue, or in some speeches, as a character to himself or to the audience, on soliloquy. (Many great poems have been cast as monologue, with poet "in character" or projecting self as a separate force.) The final type is **lyric poetry.** Although it is often removed from linear details of sequential time and action, a lyric poem will capture or paint a scene; and yet, it might contain emotional or even *dramatic* elements. Gee, have we melded these types back together? Well, there is an overlap, even controversy of classification. So, *why not revel in those conditions.*

Narrative poetry is popular with new poets, since these writers are usually employing poems to tell a story, short or long, about their lives. I did this, then I did that, then that. They did this, then that... so it goes. If the poem is interspersed with quotes, it can become, to that degree, *dramatic* poetry. Now, narrative poetry is not just for beginners— it has been a prevalent art form for thousands of years, going back to Homer and, in some cultures, even before that. Great narrative poets include: Dante, Chaucer, Spenser, Dryden, Pope, Coleridge, Byron, Longfellow, Poe, Tennyson, Browning, Kipling, Robinson, Service, (Amy) Lowell, and Kazantzakis, whose modern adaptation of Homer's *Odyssey* brings us full circle. But the fact that beginners lean on narrative verse, just as they do end-rhymes and fixed iambic meter, means the potential for mediocrity and stagnation is great. The fact is— *good* narrative poetry is very difficult to write.

The obstacles, including the time involved to tell the story, the tendency to fall into stiff, dry prose, the problems of tense and of sometimes necessary (or desirable) dialogue and monologue, *make* this difficult. Beginners may trudge along with it however, because this is primarily what they have read as poetry, and so they try to write it. "The Charge of the Light Brigade," "The Song of Hiawatha," "The Raven," "Richard Cory," "The Cremation of Sam McGee," all basic repertoire, so to speak— all narrative, and widely imitated. The fact is, these story-poems were painstakingly written by master poets, and primarily for a popular audience. They are at times exciting, beautiful, or both— and at other times, they are somewhat predictable, rhythmically singsong, and, excepting "Richard Cory" above, they are *long*. While it takes a commitment to read them, narrative poetry is, in fact, still popular and fun to write. While you will not see many pure narrative poems in today's poetry magazines and anthologies, such verse will always be part of the canon, and like many of us, I'll write some. Now, about those cliffs and rope bridges along the way.

LENGTH

There is a tendency to write and write and write narrative poems, page after page. If you are Spenser or maybe Tennyson, you get away with that. But you are not writing a *prose story*— you are writing a poem. You must still employ the "show more than tell" doctrine, or you will bore the reader. Let characterization and even some plot elements come out in scene-setting and perhaps dialogue (more on that later). One way to change-up predictability is to avoid putting in *every* sequential detail you can think of. Stick with the high spots, like jumping from stone to stone across a stream. Consider writing in short vignettes. If necessary, since scene or subject matter changes, you could *number* the vignettes. This will work in a fixed, stanzaic type of metered verse, or in free verse. But remember— SHOW more than TELL, and tell only what can't be inferred by what you show.

LANGUAGE

Don't descend into prose. With narration, you'll have to fight this tendency every step. Remember that every word counts, even those that must "tell" a fact. If you must TELL something, do it in an original way. Use metaphor and simile. Let the reader see more than the narrated plot line. Bad narrative poetry is dry, bloodless; it looks like prose cut to fit a meter (and sometimes with *very* bad rhyme). Don't let yours look like that. Honestly, until you have mastered rhyme (instead of rhyme dictating how you alter lines to fit it) you're well to consider writing your narrative poems in free verse, or blank verse (fixed meter, but unrhymed).

VOICE

In employing **the active voice,** you depict *the subject doing* ("I walk the dog") instead of, in the **passive voice,** *the object being done to* ("the dog is walked"). The former is vibrant and a staple of prose writing; the latter, simply too dull. In poetry, even more so than in prose, every word must forward its own momentum. Here, active voice *really* shoulders and delivers. Remember our early discussion of *action verbs*, and how they propel a poem's lines. *Active voice* does the same.

TENSE

Most narrative poetry is written in the *past tense*, because the poem is an account of events that happenED. Like passive versus active voice, past tense can weaken delivery, as you get caught in the spiral of *had, have been, was, etc.,* leading into your action verbs. (This is why **dialogue** enlivens prose, especially fiction; the reader is brought effortlessly from the story's past to a refreshing "present.") Tenses can otherwise be worked around, but the rest of the poem's construction must be very strong to overcome the natural, downcast lag that comes with recounting past events, including the burden of past events within *other* past events. It's like starting out of the running-blocks with a dwarf on your back. If you have to use past tense, keep it as much as possible in simple forms. (*He **ran***— NOT *he had run, he had been running, he was running, he would run,* etc.) Sometimes, you can move your poem entirely into present tense. If not, remember the present-time freshener that is *dialogue.* But whatever you do, know that your poem must be bright with images, and move quickly.

MORE ABOUT DIALOGUE

As in prose, the difficulties of creating good dialogue are the bane of the narrative poet. The poem may cry for liveliness of speech, of interplay. The poet, however, must craft this carefully. The"proser" is always tripping over the "said" words that identify the speaker. If used in moderation, and where for several lines speakers can be easily identified without use of such words, all is well. But because of the demands of poetic *economy,* one best eliminates "said" words altogether. This means your dialogue (the back and forth) should be in short spurts. While you can use quotation marks (I sometimes do), you can also use *long dashes, stanza breaks,* and *indents* to identify which character is speaking (as in the examples of "Doria" in the chapter on free verse). You can profit, too, from *dramatic monologue* or, as appropriate, from *soliloquy.* These select ribbons of verse can be unwound with insight, emotion, and detail, as in the great speeches of Shakespeare, or the arias of grand opera. Make sure, however, when you're putting words in somebody's mouth, that they really have something to say. Otherwise, get on with the story.

When comparing narrative and *lyric poetry*, it is a mistake to compartmentalize one or the other just on the basis of length. While many narrative poems are indeed long, because of the story that they tell, a *short* story could be confined to a short poem. In it, there may still be a sequence of events, but the time period could involve minutes, a week; not years, not a lifetime. Conversely, in a lyric poem and the scene it casts, a feeling or idea evoked may be so deep, so detail-oriented, as to cover hundreds of lines. The difference between narrative and lyric poetry comes by way of how time is handled *within* the poem's length, not by the length itself.

A narrative poem is *linear;* time moves by sequences of events, and in one or more settings. Characters are introduced or dispensed with as in a play. Dialogue or dramatic monologue enhance the narration with real or implied exchanges from one character to another. Via soliloquy or aside, a character talks to himself or to a reader. Time is a well-ordered, prominent accompanist— you can "mark it" throughout, whether the poem started in the past or in present time, or, at will, shuttles forward and back from the poem's beginning.

In a **lyric poem,** time is not a vehicle, nor a driving factor. Line and stanza are displayed as objects of their own, innate perfection of sight and sound, justified beyond other plan. Here, *the scene is the thing.* Time is not linear, but instantaneous. Lyric poems are snapshots, not cinema. They exist at that moment; frozen, they are flash-melted before our eyes, and the resulting pools are far deeper than they are long, or wide. This doesn't mean that we aren't taken places— *we are.* Instead of being *directed* toward a single point of destination, as in storytelling, we are *dispersed* in the explosion of image juxtaposed with other images, in musical colorations, in dynamic rhythmic pace, and ultimately, in fragments of lucid thought that are sewn together to create an entire vista.

You will see more use of metaphor and simile in a lyric poem. Unconstrained by a demand for that sequential story, the poet can fling the reader's shifting mindsets like darts in various directions— up, down, sideways through the clever use of ambiguity, and the intertwining of ideas that may seem disparate, but are they? Such ideas could have more than one meaning to the poet, and ANY NUMBER OF MEANINGS to the reader, given the reader's own feelings, thoughts, and experiences.

OR, no explanation may even be intended— just as music or painting may not be designed for specific meaning. Instead, the poem broadly emanates *mood,* allowing each recipient license to borrow the writer's expression and to go *their own way.* A lyric poem can reflect a major statement of human or spiritual beingness, or also a casual, objective understatement— from the desperate, and soon-to-be life shattering allusions of Sylvia Plath as the horse-rider in "Ariel," to the simple, it-is-what-it-is, red wheelbarrow and green glass of William Carlos Williams. Lyric poetry, as we've examined here, can be many things, or most ANYTHING. And that is why it is not only a popular means of poetic expression— it is also, in many ways, the dominant means of our day.

Now, we've shown that aspects of drama can assist both narrative *and* lyric approaches (as in the latter, spicing up a usually somber lament-genre called the *elegy*— see Donne's simmering traversals, or Poe's "Annabel Lee"). But the **dramatic poem,** isolated as its own irresistible power, foments a dynamic, externally-directed event. Through **monologue**, whether as assumed character, or self-cast as unnamed seer or demi-god, the poet moves somewhere beyond the historic, the allegoric, the elegiac, and stands before his public primed for oration and fused with feeling and concept. This poem lauds, pleads, exhorts, admonishes, scorns. Here, we elect to discard a simple musing, some slight observation, a fragmentary scene. Rather, we get emotion and thought in rapt cascade and volume.

The dramatic poem, risen from root in ancient epics, wends through works of Shakespeare, where monologues stand apart from their plays and collect as a culture's sourcebook, and scripture. Undeterred, the drama surges over centuries, winks at propriety, changes masks and arrives at the resolute declarations of Whitman and Ginsberg— as always, granting our icons license to spur, to move, to resonate.

In sum, every poet has a menu of genres and styles from which to order. Whether narrative, dramatic, or lyric, poetry is intrinsically designed to create an effect, not to languish in private journals. Our poems cry to be unlocked, listened to, and read. It is why we write poetry, regardless of the method or manner we choose.

PARALLELISM: THE ETERNAL BALANCE

From the *King James Bible:*

> To every thing there is a season,
> and a time to every purpose under the heaven:
> a time to be born, and a time to die;
> a time to plant, and a time to pluck up that which is planted;
> a time to kill, and a time to heal;
> a time to break down, and a time to build up;
> a time to weep, and a time to laugh;
> a time to mourn, and a time to dance...

It can be said that this universe depends on the existence of *two,* or *at least two* of everything. Origin and destination, yin and yang, giver and receiver, the 0 and 1 and their billion permutations inside a computer chip. So it is in written and spoken language— the subject that *is,* and the verb that *animates* it, and inevitably, the object *affected* by it. Taken further into literature and rhetoric, the concept of *duality*, of "this to that," whether in making associations or differentiations, and that conceptualize our thoughts and emotions, lay inherent in our effective writing and speech.

Such bond of *this* to *that* informs and heightens our communication and our verbal aesthetic. Both rule *and* device, the process sews word or phrase into the hem of its mate through sound or meaning, or one line into another based on specific similarity *or* difference. We call it **parallelism.** Its physics begets tension, strength, harmony, gravity, and most important, balance. Like that force which rights the child's top, or the moon-bound rocket— parallelism is engendered in the polished, vital gyroscope of our poetic utterance, and this has been so from biblical times to the second of the sentence you just read.

Rhyme and other sound devices provide parallelism *phonologically;* so does the regular rhythm of meter. This concept of balance, of building, or order, whether inherent or well-planned, extends to the repetition of phrase (the precinct of the *refrain*), to the layout of stanzas, and to other uses of space. *Syntax* orders the words in ways that cajole or direct us to make specific contacts.

Ultimately, we arrive at that which is entirely *semantic,* which conveys meaning, or varieties of meaning, to invite the reader or listener to collect information, to compare, to contrast, and to conclude in his own universe that which came from another's universe— the poet's. Somehow, this act conjoins to form that ultimate *third* universe, one of agreement or epiphany involving the other two.

While parallelism is an "issue" on which you'll be picked apart in Freshman Composition class, in that it applies to effective writing of any kind, what you'll get there is on the order of making sure you're not ignoring a correlative construction, or not mixing your gerunds with pesky infinitives. In all writing, we use parallelism as a means to effect order; it's cold-steel mechanics— syntactic precision.

But in poetry (as verse, or as oratory), parallelism transcends an effort at direct (and perfectly correct) writing or speech. Beyond it, that linking of sonic strains, objects, and ideas resets the internal and *eternal* clock of its recipient; sound now becomes *super-sound,* and meaning, both in quick effect and delayed harmonics, *becomes super-meaning.*

Consider John Keats, in "Ode on a Grecian Urn." The primary phrase of each line is bolded, its *parallel phrase,* italicized. To the side are the component *roots* of those paired phrases, be they nouns, verbs, etc.

O Attic shape! *fair attitude!* with brede	**shape**— *attitude*;
Of marble men and *maidens overwrought,*	**men**— *maidens*;
With forest branches and *the trodden weed;*	**branches**—
	weed;
Thou, silent form! **dost tease us out of thought**	**thought**—
As doth eternity: Cold Pastoral!	*eternity*;
When **old age shall this generation waste,**	**this generation**—
Thou shalt remain, in midst of other woe	*thou*;
Than ours, **a friend to man,** *to whom thou say'st,*	**to man**—
	to whom;
"Beauty is truth, *truth beauty*— that is all	**beauty / truth**—
	truth / beauty;
Ye know on earth, and all *ye need to know."*	**know**—
	need to know."

Regarding the famous couplet at the end of that example— if you go into *Bartlett's Quotations,* you'll find literally hundreds of examples where such enduring statements are based on the brilliant parallel structures within the lines.

Note, too, the "elliptical" license the poet takes throughout, departing from the standard parallelism of prose. In the following lines and in others, Keats leaves out the *formal* preposition repeats of the words "of" and "in" (bolded inside parentheses). Such deletions are allowed in the interest of flow, so long as they don't skew understanding.

Of deities or **(of)** mortals, or of both,
In Tempe or **(in)** the dales of Arcady?

Remember, writing poetry is about control, about balance, and as poet, you are the progenitor of the world you spin. Whether conscious or unconscious, these parallel structures guide both writer and reader.

Whenever you read master poetry (and you must), and now also, when you examine your own work, look within for the magic of the parallel word, the parallel phrase, the paired similarity or difference. Feel the whir of equilibrium. See the child's top upright. Hear the steady music of the spheres.

TRANSLATION: A SIDE-TRIP WORTHWHILE

Throughout the book, we discuss various measures with which poets can sharpen the ears, eyes, and mind of their writing. In addition to the ongoing (and vital) practice of *reading master poetry,* I've suggested fresh invitations to your poetic sensibility and logic—from listening to the nocturnes of Chopin, to analyzing chess games. If some of these practices have seemed a bit far afield, here's one that moves back into the province of poetry itself— **translation.**

There's no expectation that you'll become an expert translator at the outset of your poetry career, or for that matter, even at the *end* of it. It's a set-aside art, and there are many poets, Robert Frost among them, who have frowned on all attempts to translate poetry from one language to another. ("Poetry is what gets lost in translation.")

While translating languages in direct, word-for-word approximations has advanced culture beyond ancient oral traditions, and contributed to a group aesthetic that bypasses borders and tongues— the subject of *poetic translation* has remained open for debate. Certainly, there aren't many working translators out there, or even dabblers, among the master poets. Poetic translation is a specialty requiring prowess in the poet's source language, as well as in the language he has targeted. Further, the poet must be sensitive to idioms and colloquialisms of each language. For instance, the French "pomme de terre," or "apple of the earth," presents quite a different image and sound-projection than does its counterpart in English, the lowly "potato." Finally, the poet must be conscious of meter patterns prevalent in each language's poetry. Meter usually mirrors the flow of the language itself, as well as the types of consonant and vowel sounds regularly used.

Also, the *oral traditions* of a country or region may play an important part in framing the poetic art within that localized language and culture, whether in material recalled in oral (out-loud or "bardic") fashion, and delivered extemporaneously, or taken "in score" off the written page. The subject of poetic translation is obviously deep, fascinating, not a little controversial, and probably worth a full historical and linguistic accounting, with a detailed manual all its own. So why mention this subject just in passing? Well, let's look at translation as a much simpler medium, one to inspire and reinforce the poet, and to apply to the overall learning process. We'll get to that simplicity angle shortly, but first, a few more points of murky preparation.

Translation can take several forms.

One involves doing a **direct translation** that comes as close as possible to matching word meanings in both languages, while only secondarily meeting any possible demands in terms of stanza formula, syllable count or accents (as would exist in any fixed meter), or sound conventions such as rhyme. Note that because of the aforementioned differences in the speech framework of languages, as well as their natural oratorical accents and prevalent verse forms, meeting ALL goals equally and well is often an impossible challenge.

A second approach flips the considerations above, holding meter and rhyme arrangements in place, even it creates significant word (and definition) changes that affect meaning.

A *third* way, the most controversial, pushes the other approaches to the background. It uses the transformational process of metaphor, and it affirms the original poem's *figurative* message as the hallmark of the translation. This could mean a minor or MAJOR recasting of the poem among certain lines, or within every line. While the method might attempt to retain some of the previous meter or rhyme, it would more likely eliminate any of that *completely*. Here, the debate rages as to how much of the translation is actually the old poem, or an entirely NEW one. For many, Frost's point is taken.

In any event, there could be wildly different translations of the same poem from say, French into English, or English into French. Now, translating Italian into French would be easier, since both tongues are "Romance languages," using similar cadences and vowel sounds, and so affording ability to find a myriad of rhymes. Unlike the Latin-based French, Spanish, Italian and Portuguese, the English language is an amalgam of different vowel sounds and hard accents which include Anglo-Germanic influences, *plus* a bounty of *Norman-French* words brought to England by William the Conqueror. Translation of English to the *Slavic* languages can be even more difficult, because phonology and vocal inflections are both Western *and* Eastern. Add to the mix a host of colorful folk idioms, and we are challenged outright by a breadth of differing views on semantic, syntactic, and sonic order.

Given these hurdles, translators approach their job in various ways. They include: literal, or direct translation; choices of **versification** (how the verse's lines and stanzas will be composed); and *aesthetic* transformation of images or meanings apart from word-matches. The poet may translate himself, or two poets of two different languages can be involved— original writer, and new translator. A translator is free to use *any* of the approaches stated, according to his goals and preferences. But clearly, the translation of poetry is a balancing act— faithful to the original text (or poet), less so, or *much* less so.

Amazingly, poets of the target language (that language into which the source text is to be translated) may actually *collaborate* with a poet or linguist in the source language (the language of the original text), to gain from him or her a very direct translation. The *target* poet can then make the "poetic" translation into the new language.

Ezra Pound, who did not speak Chinese, relied on direct translations of the eighth century Chinese poet, Li Po, by scholar Ernest Fenollosa. Fenollosa's line-by-line translation (itself taken from character-to-character transliterations by his Japanese teachers), was combined with Pound's own piecemeal analysis of how the Chinese pictograms are constructed of multiple images and meanings. Pound proceeded to make the first real *poetic* transformations of Chinese poetry into English, and in so doing, the American master's concise, image-based flashes of language contributed much to the modern concept of free verse.

I have also attempted this particular exercise, collaborating with a Russian linguist to translate the poetry of Mayakovsky. Elsewhere, knowing French first-hand, I've translated some Rimbaud, and those translations were much more direct. I've translated a few of my own poems into French, too, a reversal of the exercise. In sum, the poet must decide the form, the accents, the sounds, the meanings, and what he or she will retain, alter, or jettison from the translation process.

Check, for instance, the opening of Canto I of Dante's *Inferno,* translated from Italian into English. The following examples leave most characteristics of that original terza rima form behind (note the lack of formal rhyme scheme), but they manage to keep the details of the narrative and, wherever possible in the difficult traverse from Italian to English, retain some of the lyric flow, if not the innate "music" of the Italian. It is in all the subtle word choices, inversions, and elaborations that the art of translation lives, and where any poet profits from **reading and comparing** such translations. *Yes, we finally reach the reason for this chapter, and how it may help you.*

Read these versions of the poem's opening segment, and note the differences, line by line.

LONGFELLOW TRANSLATION (Henry Wadsworth Longfellow, American poet, 1867)

Inferno: Canto I
(kept in tercets, but turned into blank verse)

Midway upon the journey of our life
I found myself within a forest dark,
For the straightforward pathway had been lost.

Ah me! how hard a thing it is to say
What was this forest savage, rough, and stern,
Which in the very thought renews the fear.

So bitter is it, death is little more;
But of the good to treat, which there I found,
Speak will I of other things I saw there.

CARY TRANSLATION (Henry Francis Cary, British author /
scholar, 1814)

Inferno: Canto I
(in blank verse, with an occasional end-rhyme)

In the midway of this our mortal life,
I found me in a gloomy wood, astray
Gone from the path direct: and e'en to tell
It were no easy task, how savage wild
That forest, how robust and rough its growth,
Which to remember only, my dismay
Renews, in bitterness not far from death.
Yet to discourse of what there good befell,
All else will I relate discover'd there.

NORTON TRANSLATION (Charles Eliot Norton, American
scholar / editor, 1891)

Inferno: Canto I
(in prose)

Midway upon the road of our life I found myself
within a dark wood, for the right way had been missed.
Ah! how hard a thing it is to tell what this wild and
rough and dense wood was, which in thought renews the fear! So bitter is it that death is little more.
But in order to treat of the good that there I found, I
will tell of the other things that I have seen there.

Beyond that triple comparison, I urge you to pick up the more recent translations of *The Inferno* by American poets John Ciardi (1954) and Robert Pinsky (1994), and track *them* line by line.

Now, I've offered the discourse here not to daunt or confuse, but to illustrate. The affairs of poetic communication on this level are not for the fainthearted. Sure, if you know another language well, you can always attempt a translation. And even if you aren't completely fluent in the source language— if you know someone who has made, or who can make, a *literal translation* (and is also familiar with the idioms of the language, as a native speaker would be) you could then attempt to bring that somewhat sterile "direct" translation into your own poetic transformation.

But more important is the idea of ***reading*** several existing translations of the **same work.** Spotting variations, small or large within the lines of different translations shows you the power of language in changing or retaining sound, rhythm, tone, mood, and of course, understanding.

Now, consider the decisions YOU make when writing your poems, when you are NOT translating from one language to another. Rather, you are simply trying to communicate in the best way possible, and IN ENGLISH, your own inspiration, logic, passion, and concepts that you intend to be incisive, beautiful, maybe both. Unlike the craftsmen of crossed languages, you are attempting— and you always were— to reach out to no one other than the *ENGLISH reader or listener,* who can assimilate *your* words, phrases, lines, stanzas and entire poems into *their own* consciousness. Therefore, I invite you to exercise this chapter as you will. I just hope in laying this all out that we have not lost one another— you had to know it was coming— in translation.

WHAT POETRY IS, REVISITED

At the beginning of the book, we pondered on what poetry *is*. Is it just form, or is it content; the staves, or the notes upon it. We talked about the "poetry" to be found within prose (Thomas Wolfe); in the popular song (name a songwriter you love); in oratory (Martin Luther King); even in a comedy routine (Lenny Bruce). But none of these offerings were planned as *poems*. So it is that we confuse a valid and universal concept of *poetry,* with VERSE. I think we can explore the difference better now, since we went on to view the craft of written poetry from all angles, and witnessed as well its inspiration, its intent, its music.

Like the wearer of the ruby slippers, you may not have realized at the outset, the power underfoot, the ability to go anywhere. We learn that *poetry* itself is not a solid construction but an *aesthetic wave,* one of high frequency, so high that its quantum resembles what it seeks to reflect— the ultimate concept of beauty, of innate understanding, and of a human soul. And like music and other arts operating at the subtle apex of their powers, poetry transcends the form of its vessel. It radiates, it overflows, it affects its environment, and it transcends the illusion of its appointed time. Surely, that's good enough reason to be making *any* kind of poetry, wherever one seeks and finds it.

What about VERSE? It IS form, it IS a vessel, just as the other, non-verse examples are vessels, just as musical and visual forms are vessels. But in the use of words to convey both music (sound and rhythm) and meaning (an "answer" planned or unplanned by sender to recipient), the vessel of verse, in all its interesting permutations, seems to **heighten and amplify** that wave we uncovered, making it HUM. So we learn the forms, we use the forms. And books like this get written.

I had stated that at the outset of writing a poem, I often don't figure out what form to hang it on or to contain it right away. I may start in tetrameter; soon it reshuffles into pentameter. I could begin with one rhyme scheme, end up with another, or eschew the rhymes entirely for blank verse. You'll recall I even mentioned that I will sometimes write in free verse originally, then pour the writing into a mold of one form or another to see how it might otherwise "jell." But to get off that particular metaphor and back to our reliable "Oz" musings, there are many ways one can go, this way, that way, twisting oneself about, falling down, losing straw, stuffing it back in, and heading on down the more-OR-less traveled road. And while I may tighten a form, I may also, just as easily, free it. Consider this:

CONFRATERNITY IN FREE VERSE
WITH THE GHOST OF JOHN DONNE

But as it is said
of old cosmographers, that when
they had said all that they knew of a country,
        and yet much more was to be said,
        they said
that the rest of those countries were possessed with giants,
        or witches
or spirits or wild beasts, so that
they could pierce no farther
into that country, so when
        we have traveled as far as we can, with safety,
        that is, as far as ancient, or modern expositors lead us
in the discovery
of these new heavens, and new earth,

yet we must say at last,

that it is a country inhabited with angels,

       or archangels,

with cherubim, and seraphim,

and that we can look no farther into it

with these eyes.

Where it is locally, we enquire not;

       we rest in this

that it is the habitation

prepared by the blessed saints of God,

heavens,

where the moon is more glorious than our sun,

and the Sun as glorious

       as He that made it;

for it is he himself, the son of God,

the sun of glory.

A new earth, where all

the waters are milk, and all

       their milk, honey,

where all their grass is corn

and all their corn, manna;

where all their glebe,

all their clods of earth are gold, and all

their gold of innumerable carats;

where all their minutes are ages, and all their ages, eternity;

       where every thing, is every minute

       in the highest exaltation, as good as it can be

and yet super-exalted
and infinitely multiplied by every
minute's addition, every minute
infinitely better than ever it
was before.

Of these new heavens and this new earth
we must say at last, that we
can say nothing.

For the eye of man has not seen,
nor ear heard, nor heart conceived
             the state of this place.

We limit and determine
our consideration with that horizon
with which the Holy Ghost has limited us,
that it is that new heavens
             and new earth
             wherein
dwells
righteousness.

If that poem appeared modern, yet at the same time, *anything but,*
you're on to something. I once passed out copies of this poem at a
workshop, where others proceeded to analyze it as they would any
free verse poem, and to offer suggestions. The secret of the poem was
not that I had somehow evoked the spirit of 400 year-old John Donne.
This poem IS by John Donne.

Actually, it didn't start as a Donne poem. In fact, it wasn't a *poem* at all, but a **sermon** (Donne was first a stellar, sensuous English poet, and later, an eloquent priest of the Anglican Church). To be exact, our "poem" is taken word for word from Section IV of Donne's "Sermon of Commemoration of the Lady Danvers, Late Wife of Sir John Danvers." What is amazing about this transposition of prose form to verse form, simply by use of **line breaks and space**, is that John Donne becomes for the moment, a *modern* master, rather than a Jacobean one. Now, as I had mentioned earlier, you CAN'T just put prose words into verse. There has to be high *poetic* content, *actual* poetry in that prose, or that oration, for this experiment to work. I have taken material from other unexpected places— prose passages by Wolfe, Fitzgerald, and Kerouac, a treatise by W. E. B. Du Bois, and speeches by Frederick Douglass and Abraham Lincoln, and found that all, with no alteration of the words themselves, elect their light to colors in the prism of free verse. I have even contemplated a book of such transpositions.

Poets will often find poems in odd places— for Maxine Kumin, in a travel pamphlet, for Hart Crane, in advertisements on the sides of railroad cars. Such works are classified as **found poems.** Though the words gathered may change very little if at all, the poet finds in the unintended and commonplace, something somehow enduring and sublime. Consider the still lifes of Vermeer— objects captured make objects transformed. Words are objects, beautiful; we frame them.

As with the *translation* chapter, I tell you this not for you to repeat an *exercise* (though you certainly could), but to understand the *power* you possess in arranging words— as objects claiming their own capture, or as symbols swelling of life and spirit. All that follows falls to *you,* and those slippers, too, clicking and shining the way to heaven, or home.

READING THE MASTERS

Beyond the examples you've seen throughout the book, here's a short list of poets and poetry you might read, not only for the quality of the work, but also for areas of craft in which these masters excelled. You can use any of these poets to improve those areas of your work that may apply, and revel in styles that you believe reflect, in some way, your own. I have included suggestions of specific poems, as well as poets in general over many time periods. But don't stop with those. **READ READ READ READ READ!!**— and *not only* the poets you like right now and whom you currently emulate, *but also* poets who write in TOTALLY DIFFERENT WAYS THAN YOU. This is really how you learn and inevitably, how you will find your own voice. And when you read these poets, for God's sake and whenever possible, **read the poems aloud.** They are great art; they are intoxicants. Drink them up, get drunk, LEARN.

SPECIAL NOTE: with the exception of specific types of verse such as **syllabic verse, haiku,** and **accentual verse** among what follows, the forms you'll read primarily adhere to the common and combined heading of *accentual-syllabic verse.* To review, the method classifies **metrical feet,** standard units that account for and contain groups of syllables. A foot's weak, unstressed syllables attach themselves to the dictate of strong, stressed syllables— also called "accents," or "beats."

As you may have noticed, I've lobbied for a "freeing up" of what has been *classified* as **accentual-syllabic meter.** My premise, long held, would neither deny the scansion of poetic lines, nor dictate the sole validity of the major stresses or beats. Rather, it would elevate the

stress (both the *major* stress, and by poet's decision, a *minor* stress) to relative **line dominance,** retaining a natural flow of English speech. This strategy may then alter how poetic lines are scanned to elicit their design. Already, we have approximated it. Within existing accentual-syllabic verse, categories of which are listed, many of the great poets have altered this balance between weak and strong beats intrinsically, so that the static labels have already blurred in meaning. Whitman was on this track; so were Hopkins, Sitwell, Jeffers. And in Auden, Anglo-Saxon accentual verse gained a modern champion— he was definitely on board. Eventually, I believe we'll see the refining and acknowledgment (from whom it matters, I'm not sure) of a spectrum that could unite purely accentual verse, with what for centuries has been a dominant, strictly-scanned accentual-syllabic verse. But enough about that. Here are some guideposts in the form of various poets, specific poems, and larger works or collections *(in italics)* placed for you by type or subject matter for what must, in the end, be a private and self-illuminating journey:

USE OF METAPHOR AND SIMILE:
works of Jalalud'din Rumi (tr. Persian);
works of William Shakespeare;
works of John Donne, especially "The Flea";
John Keats — "Ode on a Grecian Urn," "The Eve of St. Agnes";
Charles Baudelaire (tr. French)— *Flowers of Evil*;
Arthur Rimbaud (tr. French)—"The Drunken Boat";
works of Rainer Maria Rilke (tr. German);
Hart Crane— *The Bridge*;
Hyman J. Sobiloff — "Knock-Knock," "Delphic";
Marge Piercy— "Putting the Good Things Away";
Robert Bly— *Iron John*;

Anne Sexton— *Transformations;*

James Wright— "Autumn Begins in Martin's Ferry, Ohio";

Richard Wilbur— "Love Calls Us to the Things of This World."

USE OF SOUND (consonance, assonance, rhythm, etc.):

John Dryden— "A Song for St. Cecilia's Day";

Percy Bysshe Shelley—"To a Skylark";

Gerard Manley Hopkins—"As Kingfishers Catch Fire";

Vachel Lindsay—"The Congo";

Hart Crane— "At Melville's Tomb";

Dylan Thomas— "A Refusal to Mourn the Death, by Fire, of a Child in London," "Fern Hill";

James Merrill— "The Black Swan";

Robert Hayden— "Those Winter Sundays";

works of Langston Hughes.

USE OF IRONY AND UNDERSTATEMENT:

Alexander Pope— "The Rape of the Lock";

Percy Bysshe Shelley— "Ozymandias";

Dorothy Parker— "Unfortunate Coincidence," "Resume";

Ogden Nash— "Portrait of the Artist as a Prematurely Old Man";

Stevie Smith— "Not Waving But Drowning";

works of Pablo Neruda (tr. Spanish);

John Berryman— *The Dream Songs;*

Gwendolyn Brooks— "The Independent Man";

Anne Sexton— "The Little Peasant," "The Truth the Dead Know."

USE OF DIALOGUE / MONOLOGUE:

William Shakespeare (the plays);

works of Robert Browning;

T.S. Eliot— "The Waste Land."

SHORT LINES (quick poems that strike the eye)**:**

works of William Blake;

William Carlos Williams (later work);

works of Emily Dickinson;

James Emanuel— "Negro";

Sylvia Plath (later work— the *Ariel* poems).

LONG LINES (creating horizontal tension, then release)**:**

Walt Whitman— *Leaves of Grass;*

Allen Ginsberg— "Howl."

SONNET FORM:

collection of Petrarch (Francesco Petrarca) (tr. Italian);

collection of William Shakespeare;

collection of John Donne;

Dante Gabriel Rossetti— *The House of Life.*

RHYMED METER (pentameter, tetrameter, etc.)**:**

John Donne— "The Ecstasy";

Alexander Pope— "The Rape of the Lock";

William Blake— *Songs of Innocence and Experience;*

Percy Bysshe Shelley— "Ode to the West Wind";

W. B. Yeats— "The Tower," "September 1913";

John Keats— "Ode on a Grecian Urn," "The Eve of St. Agnes," "Ode to a Nightingale."

BALLAD FORM:
Samuel Taylor Coleridge— "Rime of the Ancient Mariner";
works of Robert Burns;
Oscar Wilde— "The Ballad of Reading Gaol."

ACCENTUAL VERSE (driven solely by accents, wherever
they fall, or often, in fixed numbers or placements per line)**:**
Anonymous (tr. Old English [Anglo-Saxon])— "Beowulf"
(as translated by Seamus Heaney);
Thomas Wyatt— "Whoso List to Hunt";
Samuel Taylor Coleridge— "Christabel";
Walt Whitman— *Leaves of Grass* (major experiments and
modern advances utilizing accentual cadences previously
found in the English Bible);
Gerard Manley Hopkins— "Grendel" (an example of
Hopkins's inventive "sprung rhythm");
Rudyard Kipling— "Harp Song of the Dane Women";
works of Edith Sitwell;
W. H. Auden— "The Age of Anxiety" (Anglo-Saxon-style
accentual meter— 4 accents per line, brief pause in middle of
each line, 3 of the accents in each line display alliteration);
Richard Wilbur— "Junk."

SYLLABIC VERSE (where a strict syllable count controls
the lines— *not* the stresses)**:**
Robert Bridges— "The Testament of Beauty";
Dylan Thomas— "In My Craft, or Sullen Art";
Marianne Moore— "Poetry," "The Mind is an Enchanted
Thing;"
Thom Gunn— "Considering the Snail."

CLASSICAL VERSE: (accents based on syllable length):

Homer (tr. Greek)— *The Iliad, The Odyssey;*

works of Sappho (tr. Greek);

works of Pindar (tr. Greek);

works of Catullus (tr. Latin);

Virgil (tr. Latin)— *The Aeneid* (as translated by John Dryden or Ezra Pound);

works of Horace (tr. Latin);

Ovid (tr. Latin)— *Metamorphoses* (as translated by John Dryden or Ted Hughes).

BLANK VERSE (regular meter, unrhymed):

William Shakespeare— many of the plays (which contain some of the greatest poetry in the English language);

John Milton— *Paradise Lost;*

William Wordsworth— "Lines Composed a Few Miles Above Tintern Abbey";

Robert Frost— "Mending Wall";

Stephen Spender— "The Express";

Wallace Stevens— "The Idea of Order at Key West."

FREE VERSE:

This area is probably too broad to categorize well; you will find aspects of it— with specific texts set apart from metrical form— going back to the Bible and the oral roots of poetry. But for our purposes, the epoch of free verse begins with Walt Whitman's *Leaves of Grass,* and what is considered the dawn of *modern poetry.* (Note that Whitman, as we've indicated, emphasized the accents of natural speech; otherwise, the poet altogether freed his lines of fixed length and regular sound.)

Stephen Crane wrote searing poems in free verse. Ezra Pound further developed it as a genre. T. S. Eliot assured its academic acceptance with "The Love Song of J. Alfred Prufrock" and his masterpiece, "The Waste Land." William Carlos Williams, in *Paterson,* and Charles Olson, in "The Kingfishers," rejected Eliot's "metaphysical" approach to it. Gertrude Stein aurally diced and cubed its language; E. E. Cummings scattered its lines like pigeons on the page, while Allen Ginsberg and the Beats filled its voice with politics and social commentary, as exemplified by "Howl." Confessional poets Robert Lowell, Sylvia Plath, and Anne Sexton condensed its clarion call into focused, personal asides. Today, poets everywhere push and pull it in all directions. Start anywhere; read LOTS of the *best* of it. A sea between shores, free verse awaits your voyage.

PHILOSOPHICAL VERSE (deep concepts, on the condition of the world, humanity, life and death):
works of Jalalud'din Rumi (tr. Persian);
Dante (tr. Italian)— *The Divine Comedy;*
George Herbert— "The Pulley," "Vanity (I)";
John Milton— *Paradise Lost;*
Andrew Marvell— "The Definition of Love";
T. S. Eliot— "The Love Song of J. Alfred Prufrock,"
"The Waste Land," "The Hollow Men";
Wallace Stevens— "The Idea of Order at Key West,"
and indeed, like Eliot, virtually all of his work;
Conrad Aiken— "Tetélestai";
works of Pablo Neruda (tr. Spanish);
works of W. H. Auden;
Robert Lowell— "For the Union Dead."

SENSUAL, ECSTATIC VERSE:

works of John Donne;

William Blake— *The Book of Thel, The Book of Los*, etc.

Samuel Taylor Coleridge— "Kubla Khan";

Charles Baudelaire (tr. French)— *Flowers of Evil*;

works of Paul Verlaine (tr. French);

works of Vladimir Mayakovsky (tr. Russian);

Stephen Crane— "In the Desert," "I Saw a Man";

Arthur Rimbaud (tr. French)— "The Drunken Boat";

Hart Crane— "Lachrymae Christi," "Voyages II."

NARRATIVE POEMS (telling a sequential story):

Dante (tr. Italian)— *The Divine Comedy*;

Alfred Lord Tennyson—"The Lady of Shalott";

Lord Byron (George Gordon)— *Don Juan;*

Edward Arlington Robinson—"Richard Cory";

Robert Service— "Jean Desprez";

Nikos Kazantzakis (tr. Greek)— *The Odyssey.*

SESTINA:

Ezra Pound— "Sestina: Alaforte";

Anthony Hecht— "Sestina d'Inverno."

VILLANELLE:

William Empson— "Missing Dates";

Dylan Thomas— "Do Not Go Gentle into That Good Night."

POLITICAL OR WAR POEMS:

John Dryden—"Absalom and Achitopel: A Poem";

Percy Bysshe Shelley— "England in 1819";

Wilfred Owen— "Anthem for Doomed Youth," "Greater Love," "Mental Cases";
Robert Service— *Rhymes of a Red Cross Man*;
Lawrence Ferlinghetti—"Tentative Description of a Dinner to Impeach President Eisenhower";
Muriel Ruykeyser— "In Our Time," "Despisals";
Amiri Inamu Baraka (Leroi Jones)— "The New World."

CONFESSIONAL POEMS:
Sylvia Plath—"Daddy";
Theodore Roethke— "I Knew a Woman";
Allen Ginsberg— "Kaddish";
Robert Lowell— "Memories of West Street and Lepke";
Adrienne Rich— "Twenty-One Love Poems."

NATURE POEMS:
Marianne Moore— "The Pangolin," "The Fish";
Elizabeth Bishop—"The Fish" (a different poem from Moore's), "The Armadillo";
works of Robinson Jeffers;
works of Mary Oliver.

POEMS OF LOVE AND PASSION:
William Shakespeare— Sonnets 18, 71, 116;
John Donne— "To His Mistress Going to Bed";
John Keats— "The Eve of St. Agnes";
Elizabeth Barrett Browning, *Sonnets from the Portuguese:* Sonnets 1 and 43;
Edna St. Vincent Millay— "Recuerdo";
Galway Kinnell— "Last Gods."

CONCRETE POEMS (shape and graphic-based):
George Herbert— "The Altar," "Easter Wings";
works of E. E. Cummings;
works of Ezra Pound, including parts of *The Cantos;*
works of Eugen Gomringer.

HAIKU:
works of Matsuo Basho (as translated by Robert Hass);
Ezra Pound— "In a Station of the Metro";
Jack Kerouac— *Mexico City Blues.*

LIGHT AND / OR SIMPLE VERSE:
In this section, we bypass verse of "inspirational" or greeting
card variety, such as that of Edgar Guest, Helen Steiner Rice,
Rod McKuen, and Susan Polis Schutz, leaving it to its own
audience. Instead, we point you to "accessible" poetry that,
while easy-to-read, leavens ambition in its delivery of sound,
image, timeless thought, and meaning, as exemplified by:

works of Emily Dickinson;
works of Rudyard Kipling;
Edgar Lee Masters— *Spoon River Anthology*;
works of Stephen Crane;
Robert Frost— "After Apple Picking," "The Road Not
Taken";
works of Dorothy Parker;
Carl Sandburg— "Chicago";
works of Edna St. Vincent Millay;
works of Robert Service;
works of John Ciardi.

Depending on the translation, poems of Pablo Neruda could enter this category— amazing, because you could place him (and I did, earlier) with the most complex poets on other terms. While we're at it, some of the "deepest" verse extant is some of the oldest, and even in translation from its native Italian, still quite easy to read. By this, we mean *The Inferno* and other books that comprise Dante's *The Divine Comedy.* So, if you like, you can read *simple,* even as you read deep. For clever, humorous verse consider works of Lewis Carroll, Edward Lear, E. E. Cummings, and Ogden Nash.

POETRY IN POPULAR MUSIC:

I cannot move on without acknowledging the fact that many young poets get their start listening to the beautiful or profound lyrics of certain popular songs. While songwriting itself is a pursuit separate from poetry, there are certainly many popular songwriters in whose work, here and there, the two endeavors overlap, and exist in a complete harmony of art and craft. (In the days of the Homeric bards and later, in the time of the troubadours and Francois Villon, there was actually no separation to all this— it was one art, one craft, not two in sympathy.) When browsing a list of the popular songwriters whose work might exemplify that premise of song as poetic expression, many artists qualify. But to me, only three transcend to recognition as exemplars of written poetry. They are: Leonard Cohen, Joni Mitchell, and especially, Bob Dylan.

For Cohen, who has also authored several books of "straight" poetry, I would recommend his first album, *Songs of Leonard Cohen.* For Mitchell, her 1971 album, *Blue.* With Dylan, the body of stellar work is enormous. And Dylan's acolytes are telling— in addition to Cohen and Mitchell themselves, they include poets Michael McClure and Allen Ginsberg; Andrew Motion, who succeeded Ted Hughes as England's Poet Laureate; playwright Sam Shepard; and amazingly, the renowned Eliot and Keats scholar Christopher Ricks— all of whom consider Dylan one of the finest American poets of the past half-century. And so do I. Try the albums *Bringing It All Back Home, Highway 61 Revisited, Blonde on Blonde, John Wesley Harding, Blood on the Tracks* (his finest single collection), *Infidels,* and *Time Out of Mind.* Such belief in Dylan provokes controversy, but controversy in the world of poetry has always been good for the art. See what *you* think.

Boy, making lists takes a while when it comes to suggesting byroads for more than a millennium of written poetry. What's here just scratches the surface, of course— there could have been pages more of recommendations. But you have to start *somewhere.* Beyond building a permanent collection of the master poets, you can always seek them out at one the many deep-resource internet sites, such as the venerable **www.poetryfoundation.org** and **www.poets.org**— or, for a clearly *anti-establishment* take on the academic poetry scene, as well as fearless, brilliant assessments of many poets, including the famous, with which you may or may not agree (again, it's informed debate that spurs our progress)— try Dan Schneider's **www.cosmoetica.com**.

Whatever you do— read. READ. Read the master poets. ALOUD when possible. Read your contemporaries. Read more than you write. And then write more than you do now, so that someday, you'll be on someone's list, too.

MASTER POETS IN THEIR OWN VOICE

In other chapters, we've covered various resources that can make a poet better, quickly. Over and again, we've stressed the importance of reading poetry, especially master poetry. Supporting this comes an additional instruction, if not order: seek out and listen to the finest poets of the past century READING ALOUD THEIR OWN WORK. These recordings are the living, sonic testaments of poems you have read, or meant to. Works will open up to you as if new when you hear them read aloud in the cadences and dynamics of their authors. Like Stravinsky conducting his own *Rite of Spring,* or Rachmaninoff playing his own *Third Piano Concerto,* hearing a work of art delivered by its creator is both an enlightening and humbling experience. True, some poems are best taken in thoughtful steps off the page, and this is necessary where space or graphic form are important. Otherwise— we celebrate an ability to reclaim the words, lines, and evocations of our chosen mediums from the figurative heaven-or-hell through which the poems came. We *restore* their sound, rhythm, emphasis, understatement or bombast, and forge an act of communion that is both must and pleasure for every poet who would fully appreciate those masters, and all they have to offer as distant, even long-dead mentors.

Take, for instance, T. S. Eliot. For any poet or savorer of Eliot's lofty and transcendent gift, reading "The Waste Land" is an imposing task, like walking up Everest. You want to do it, you trudge the slopes with Sherpas carrying your bags, only to find, gee, the air is thin up here, the incline so steep. And you climb over and over, dizzied by the effect, *over and over,* providing you don't give up. But when you put Eliot in your cassette-or-disc player reading his own version from 1958, it's a different trip altogether. The first thing that strikes you is

Eliot's mild, patrician delivery. It may sound just too mannered at first, but keep listening. In it you will feel every slight change in dynamic, loud and soft, the rhythm elastic, like rubato on a piano. The poet also displays a nifty penchant for assuming roles in several short, dramatic monologues he creates. Improbably, I have heard the great orator / actor Alec Guinness read this poem, and it did nothing for me. Eliot's own recording, however— I've listened to it perhaps 100 times, and in so doing, learned as much about my *own* world, as I did about his.

The same can be said for Eliot's first great poem, "The Love Song of J. Alfred Prufrock"— try reading it aloud yourself, and then put Eliot on— a revelation occurs. And the poet's *Four Quartets* really become *musical* quartets in hands (and voice) of his reading. Eliot's own recordings of his work have always been available, first on LP, then cassette— and now on CDs, from Random House Audio Voices (about $15.00) and Harper Collins Audio Books (about $12.00).

Another must-have is the collection (on cassette) of Anne Sexton's work, from Harper / Caedmon Audio ($13.00). In many ways, Sexton was poetry's rock star— a tough, earthy, brilliant and brutally honest confessional poet, and the finest female reader of her generation. Such piercing humor, irony, sexual edge, and ultimately, devastation, can be heard nowhere else— even in the beautiful diction of Sylvia Plath, also on Harper / Caedmon Audio (about $13.00).

Of course, the father of orated poetry is Dylan Thomas. The set of his complete recorded work for the Caedmon record label (prefaced by Billy Collins) is still available from Caedmon— and cheap enough to provoke a sense of comic disbelief— **under $30.00** for an **11-CD set** worth ten-fold the price! The hard-drinking Welshman was the single greatest dramatic reader of poetry who ever lived; and here he is, reading hour upon hour of his oeuvre, some of the most sonically-enriched poetry ever written.

Regarding extensive *audio anthologies* of master poets reading their own work, four are of note:

1. *The Caedmon Poetry Collection: A Century of Poets Reading Their Work*— 3 CDs comprise recorded work of 36 poets, many of whom I originally heard on scratchy Caedmon records played by a very fine English teacher— and the man to whom this book is dedicated— almost four decades ago. Many of the greats are here: Yeats, Stein, Frost, Pound, Sitwell, MacLeish, Auden, Spender, (Robert) Lowell, Sexton— and it concludes with the storied, 434-line masterpiece of modern poetry: T. S. Eliot's "The Waste Land" (about $20.00).

2. Rhino Word Beat's *In Their Own Voices: A Century of Recorded Poetry*— features 76 poets from the past 100 years. Of these, the most arresting segments: Dylan Thomas again, at the peak of his oratory power; the florid audacity of Edna St. Vincent Millay; W. H. Auden's cool command; the over-the-top brogue of W. B. Yeats; the standup comic approaches of Allen Ginsberg and Charles Bukowski; the wry elegance of Adrienne Rich; the earnest candor of Muriel Rukeyser; the quiet beauty of Lisel Mueller; the raspy incantations of Robert Frost. They're all here (save for Eliot), a cross-section of our culture going all the way back to an Edison cylinder purported to be Walt Whitman, circa 1890! (Now out of print, but available used for $20.00 to $50.00.) NOTE: Volumes of *single poets* from these sets— for instance, Frost, Auden, and Wilbur on Random House CDs, or Pound and Moore on Harper / Caedmon cassettes— are available from $12.00 to $22.00.

3. Sourcebooks MediaFusion's **Poetry Speaks (Expanded)**— a hard-cover book plus 3-CD set covers 47 master poets, from Alfred Lord Tennyson (!) to Sylvia Plath. Poems are introduced by other poets; the book includes the text of all the poems read, plus bios, critical commentary, personal photos, and photographed artifacts (about $30.00).

4. Shout! Factory's *Poetry on Record: 98 Poets Read Their Work (1888-2006)*— the newest of the group, features poets as far back as Robert Browning (another *amazing* find), explores the high points of modern recorded poetry of the early and mid-twentieth century, then moves to an ample representation of poets from the 1960s, and ends its survey well past the year 2000. You'll find such still-contemporary poets as Seamus Heaney, James Tate, Anne Waldman, Rita Dove, and Elise Paschen— plus recent poets selected from various branches of ethnic poetry, including the Pan African, Puerto Rican (Nuyorican), Chicano, Asian, and Native American communities (about $30.00).

With those four big anthologies, there are naturally some overlaps in poems covered, but not enough for me not to recommend all four.

For poetry from a time *before* tape recorders, you have to make do with excellent substitute readers (sometimes famous actors, sometimes not) reading poetry from the Elizabethan to the Romantic eras. While good collections of this material have been only spottily available in the past decade, the budget classical music label Naxos has launched an excellent series of classic novel and poetry readings that includes Shakespeare, the Romantics (Wordsworth, Byron, Shelley, Keats, etc.), and Milton's *Paradise Lost.* Also, if you can find any CDs, tapes, or even old records of actor Richard Burton reading Dylan Thomas, John Donne, or Shakespeare's *Hamlet*— grab them. They are all fabulous.

Regarding Shakespeare— all the plays are available in various media. For me, the *monologues* within the plays remain not only touchstones of our culture, but also a collective force within our poetic art. Any poet of *any* style who has not absorbed to his toes the great works of Shakespeare cheats himself of the knowledge of his own craft, and the vital nature of his vocation. On that note, here's a breathtaking audio library of scenes and monologues delivered by: Gielgud, Barrymore, Richardson, Guinness, Olivier, Burton, Scofield, Lesser, Ashcroft, Anderson, et al., in a 6-CD set from Rhino / Word Beat titled *Be Thou Now Persuaded: Living in a Shakespearean World* (about $40.00).

Finally, I must mention a remarkable series of VHS tapes called *Voices and Visions*, an audio-visual compendium of the life and work of thirteen great American poets: Walt Whitman, Emily Dickinson, Robert Frost, Hart Crane, Marianne Moore, Ezra Pound, T. S. Eliot, William Carlos Williams, Langston Hughes, Wallace Stevens, Elizabeth Bishop, Robert Lowell and Sylvia Plath. Equal parts detailed biography, cogent criticism, and actual performance by the poets themselves, I can think of no better single resource for exposure to the craft, history, and perspectives of modern poetry. Little wonder the series has been around for years on public television, and is frequently included in the curriculum of college English and humanities courses. While those original VHS tapes have gone out of print, a set of DVDs is still available as of this writing from **www.learner.org.**

Don't wait. Start building your audio poetry collection today. The more you listen, the more you will absorb the cadences, music, and inner meaning of the best artistic creations and creators this culture has to offer— our greatest poets, and their specially-captured legacy to the great poets that must follow them— maybe you.

A POET'S LIBRARY

It's time you gave yourself some important book resources. Budget as you must (and you can certainly find used copies at better prices than those listed), but build a *library* of these items. They are:

Judson Jerome— *The Poet's Handbook*— about $16.00 — the best single volume of poetic instruction you will ever find. Easy to read, easy to get into and not put down. And once through it, you will go back to it again and again.

Thorndike-Barnhart (or similar good, working) *Dictionary*— about $35.00. You need a *very good* dictionary to consult regularly— not to fish for words that sound "poetic" (heaven forbid), but to make sure you're using the words you *have* selected *correctly*. Is that word you want to use *exactly* correct in definition? Is there a reason, much as you might like a word, to shelve it? The dictionary is your safeguard, and a good, deep one will be the best friend you have. Pick one with extensive definitions, covering every possible use— important so that you won't assume a WRONG USAGE in the context you've selected. As further confirmation that you've selected properly, choose, as in the *Thorndike*, a dictionary that will show you the DERIVATIONS OF WORDS— where a word came from and what root definitions existed before the word was strained through various secondary languages and usages. You will be surprised how much certainty the derivation of a word can give you.

The Norton Anthology of Modern and Contemporary Poetry—
2 vols., about $50.00. Poetry that has mattered for the last century-plus. Nearly 200 poets, over 1500 poems of various genres and motifs

that you must see and at least in part, absorb. In the panorama of 2000 or so pages, you'll find the Himalayas of the culture in which we live, its air thinned with controversies of style, but indispensable. You'll go back to it often— it WILL NOT just sit on your shelf. One the biggest problems poets have— and we bemoan this always— they don't read master poetry. Crazy, and true, but certainly not you! This set, newly revised (though I prefer the older, single edition), remains the most important collection of modern poetry, from Whitman to the present.

The Norton Anthology of Poetry— about $45.00— Different from the other *Norton*— it covers English poetry from its origins through and *into* modern poetry. About a quarter of the book mirrors the other— yet don't let that keep you from this anthology. You require the assets of English poetry's previous centuries, too— not merely for historical perspective, but also for a full exploration of the past's sonic clarity, its command of form, and its brilliance of metaphor. While certain elements of craft hit their peaks before the era of Walt Whitman, the legacy of prior centuries of poetry continues to influence our art to this day. For those who specialize in formal verse, this collection becomes essential; in that case, the relative places of the two *Norton* volumes swap accordingly. Of course, we think every poet should have BOTH books, and read from them again and again— especially ALOUD.

Robert Pinsky— *The Sounds of Poetry; A Brief Guide*— about $9.00 (in paperback)—As you have likely guessed during our walk through the chapters of *On Writing Poetry,* I've long held that a poet's cognizance of sound and its devices is vital; yet, this force has been bled from poetry over the past century, to the detriment of the art. So Pinsky's focus on **sound** in this, his primer, becomes must-reading.

Poet's Market— about $25.00— When you are ready to submit for publishing (more on this in succeeding chapters), this is the resource you will use. Until you *are* ready, peruse it to stoke your desire to work, to hone your poetry so that you *will* be ready soon. Just looking at those 1000-plus markets, with all their varied potential, is enough to turn embers orange. Once you start submitting, you'll want to pick up a new *Poet's Market* every year. (New editions for the next year come out every September or so.)

Michael J. Bugeja— ***The Art and Craft of Poetry***— about $8.00 (in paperback)— Mentioned earlier, this is another excellent primer for poets. Where Judson Jerome uses light essays and examples to cover the necessary material, Bugeja goes deeper, and employs many interesting exercises for poets to explore. Between Jerome and Bugeja, certainly all bases are covered, from two slightly different points of view. (By the way, the late Judson Jerome was, for years, the Poetry Columnist for *Writer's Digest*. Michael J. Bugeja was his successor.)

Lewis Turco— ***The Book of Forms: A Handbook of Poetics***— about $20.00 (in paperback)— Noted poet-scholar Lewis Turco covers every conceivable form and variant. This book isn't light reading; it wasn't meant to be. It's a true *reference book* compiled by a poet who lives and breathes *forms.* For the working "formalist" poet, or for the novice who wants to explore formal verse of all kinds, the handbook will be a welcome, perhaps invaluable companion.

The Princeton Encyclopedia of Poetry and Poetics— about $25.00— Anything and everything you want to know about the history of poetry and poetic construction (prosody), from anywhere, from any time. A large, thick volume that will be especially helpful to those who dabble in esoteric forms, or who want to assimilate a worldwide poetic perspective. Comprehensive— and occasionally dry, depending on the contributor— this is a "go-to" volume; *endlessly* useful.

Edward Johnson— *The Handbook of Good English*— about $15.00— You need this or some other good grammar / usage book, of which there are plenty. With the exception of some fragmentary free verse (and only that which might carry sufficient other merits to supplant the normal flow of the English language) grammar is NOT suspended in good poetry. The Johnson primer is breezily written, and is not laid out like a text book. If you prefer a systematic, instructional feel, the great *Warriner's* grammar book you may have used in middle grades and high school would do nicely. Other possibilities, carrying $20.00-$30.00 price tags, are *Fowler's Modern English Usage,* and *The Chicago Manual of Style.*

***The Compact Edition of the Oxford English Dictionary*—** about $350.00, with reading glass, or $250.00 as a CD-ROM— This tome is, for us, the final arbiter and deepest single resource on the written English word. The *Compact Edition* takes the TWENTY normal-print volumes of the *Oxford English Dictionary* and reduces them to 2400 pages, where you need that elegant glass to view an entry! But it's ALL there— the entire language— all the words, definitions, usages, derivations; plus every archaic, specialized, colloquial, slang, and outright dirty word ever uttered and recorded by an English human. Certainly not your everyday, working dictionary, the "OED" remains a wildly useful, luxurious insurance policy— if you can afford it.

***Bartlett's Familiar Quotations*—** about $20.00— A fine quotation can launch your poem or affirm its point of view. Many such quotes, as you'll find perusing this comprehensive collection of memorable lines by famous and not-so-famous people, can give you ideas for new poems. Lots of humor, irony, and great wisdom in these pronouncements. Lots to use.

T. S. Eliot's "The Waste Land" in Facsimile— about $16.00— From the original manuscript with editing notes by Ezra Pound— an insight into the drafting and editing process of arguably the greatest poetic work of modern times. The original typed pages of Eliot's working drafts were photographed, transcribed for clarity, and annotated, with all the edits and margin notes of Eliot and Ezra Pound left intact. While Pound was a fine poet and to most, a modern master, he was also, perhaps, poetry's supreme editor. This large trade paperback will enhance a poet's ideas about the processes of re-drafting and editing, essential to anyone's development. That such a painstaking process was documented for THIS poem, for this monument of poetic literature, makes the experience of reliving and learning from this specific act of creation a prerequisite for any poet who aspires to competence, let alone greatness. The most interesting results of Eliot's process, as guided by Pound, are shown in passages ultimately *left out* of the opus. Conversely, you see that in the original draft, the final section of "The Waste Land" HAS NO SUGGESTED EDITS, a deliberate act of restraint by Pound. Pound felt that at that point, Eliot was in such a zone of perfection as to make ANY edit futile. And he was right.

Voices and Visions: The Poet in America (Companion to the PBS Series)— about $10.00 used, or might still be purchased new (from a college bookstore) for about $60.00 — An excellent volume that was written as a textbook companion to the already recommended *Voices and Visions*, a documentary TV series used as part of the English or humanities curriculum of many colleges. The beautifully produced biographical / critical series focuses on thirteen great American poets from Walt Whitman to Sylvia Plath, and the book, containing much additional material, is a tremendous resource of poetic craft and perspective, even without the series at hand.

An adult-level **encyclopedia** (set, or compact volume)— Great for checking your facts— and necessary for science, arts or historical poems, as well as a terrific starting point for poem ideas. (As a kid, I spent *hours* reading encyclopedias, since they could take me just about anywhere I wanted to go.) My favorite encyclopedia sets could be yours, too— *Britannica, Americana,* or *Colliers.* A set can cost a great deal of course, but you can usually find used sets for ten cents or less on the dollar. A large, single (compact) volume will cost in the $40.00 to $50.00 range. There are many good compacts available— for instance, the one from *Random House.*

AND THE FOLLOWING BOOKS YOU WILL NOT NEED:

A *thesaurus.* (Unless you also write prose.) In prose, the writer must often dwell on a piece of subject matter because of the necessity of explaining details; for that, a thesaurus such as *Roget's* becomes a very useful tool. But for poetry, no. Poets dwell too much as it is; move off your word, move on with your subject. If you find yourself constantly looking for a synonym for a word you've already used, it's a sign your poem is just not moving. Remember that poems are vertical entities— they flow as if by gravity. Searching for synonyms (which after all, are words NOT exactly identical to your favorite word anyway) means you are trying to invent hovering machines that will crash as in those funny old newsreels. No, use a word once, and move your poem on. And leave your thesaurus for a term paper.

A *rhyming dictionary.* If you use one of these regularly, no, at all, I disown you. Anyone engaging the devil and his rhyming dictionary has betrayed sonic instinct for external sampling, akin to Aunt Celia's myna bird, waiting for a Ritz. If a rhyme doesn't come to you within your own private creative process, within the context and flow of the poem, the odds are it will be a rhyme that adds nothing to the picture the poem paints, and worse, will probably throw the poem off the tracks altogether. You might as well run through the alphabet in your head— no, don't do that either. Trust yourself, and your vision, without falling back to Jiffy instant muffin mixes, to insidious crutches. REPEAT— DON'T USE A RHYMING DICTIONARY. I'll come to your house and grab it, I swear.

COPYRIGHTS AND THE THEFT OF RAINBOWS

Many poets have questions about copyrights. Now, if you were publishing a novel, a screenplay, a nonfiction book, a manual, or even a full collection of poetry, copyrights have their place. Where they do not particularly have a place is with copyright "tags" tacked on to individual poems, whether posted on the internet or submitted to print magazines. Really, who wants to steal your poem? If they did, what could they *do* with it? While you may cherish it, and while a reader may love it also (once read), a poem has the same value as a sunset in Bimini, a rainbow, an ice cream cone, or a kiss. Value? Yes. *Market value* (i.e., can you put it in a bottle and sell it)? No. (Well, I guess you CAN sell kisses, but it takes all the fun out.)

Should this fear of poetry thieves apply to you or someone you know, smell the lilacs. Some of the greatest poets of our generation sell an average of 5,000 copies of their newest collections. While yes, those books are copyrighted, do you see that what you or I *routinely* post or submit we needn't worry a whole lot about? The numbers in the equation betray the odds of your having a problem protecting your work. Sure, when you go to publish your collection, you will copyright it in an official-looking way. Until then, fall off your high horse. Poetry is important, but it is NOT serious. I have never copyrighted an *individual* poem, and never labeled a poem "Copyright 20__, Al Rocheleau," in all the years I've been writing. (Others have added that label when a poem of mine appeared online in their area, but anything beyond *my name* wasn't my idea.) Frankly, it's silly.

Now of course, that doesn't mean YOU have to think that way. If you truly feel somebody's going to steal your work, then go ahead and put the little *Copyright 20__, Jane Doe,* after the pieces you post. Just know that it drives a lot of us nuts when we see that.

It's a basic tenet of copyright law that if you put your creative work on paper you are, in effect, already protected by a copyright. (The official copyright "tag" you attach at the end may "warn" others that you will defend this work as yours, but really—defend what, to whom, and how?) By the way, I might very well put a copyright tag, and perhaps even register important work officially if I were SONG-WRITING, because songs *can* have market value, and there lay a possible issue. Likelihood aside, songs could and have been stolen, although it is more often the *tunes* that get "borrowed" than the lyrics. Anyhow, we're not talking songs here, we're talking POEMS, and there IS a difference. If you think your poems could be put to music, then go for your copyright. Otherwise, take it easy.

Understand that when working poets spy that copyright stuff under a poem, we think, "oooh, a SERIOUS poet. Not at all like us." Now, if you submit to print magazines or journals and use that copyright line, they will KNOW you are an amateur, and it will turn them off to the point of not even *reading* your poem, let alone using it. What I just said is fact; take it to the bank, cash the check.

When and if your poem is put into a publication, it is *automatically* copyrighted *for you* by that magazine as part of the issue, after which all rights to the poem are usually returned to you. Of course, the only real value this affair carries is that you now have a "credit" to add to the cover letters of other submissions, or to the "credits page" of some future collection in which the poem appears, citing the magazine that first published it. In any case, the significance of such copyrighting is still as profound as is the possibility of your opus being pinched and and pawned by a poetic cat burglar. And that is: unlikely.

Now, about concepts of **"fair use," copying style of, being inspired by, etc.** Poets may, consciously or unconsciously pick up a word or phrase here or there, and use it in a new piece. Happens all the time, to everyone, to and from. Eliot once said— and you might remember the quote—"Immature poets imitate; mature poets steal." He does not, of course, mean steal whole poems. And Eliot, perhaps the greatest of all modern poets, was an inveterate thief. Yes, he would frequently footnote his poems, sometimes laboriously, citing where he picked the pocket of Shakespeare, or Marvell, or Dante— *but not always.* If you are, quite obviously making use of something, footnoting is not a bad idea. You could begin a poem with a quote by someone, noting who said it. Truly though, the best poets LOVE to be stolen from. They know what it means, and it flatters the hell out of them.

To be sure, hundreds of poets rob from Eliot, Dickinson, Ginsberg, and Plath every day. The frightening proposition, however, is that more poets, hordes of them, steal from "greeting card poets" whose pretty books clutter your local bookstore, pushing out Shakespeare, Marvell, Dante, AND Eliot. Oh well. Suffice to say that you're able to copyright your pieces immediately by *just writing them down,* not by putting that silly little tag at the end, which, like labels on the backs of seat cushions, should not be removed under penalty of somebody's puffed-up law. If you're REALLY worried (and songwriters may be), you can write to the ***Copyright Office of the Library of Congress*** in Washington D.C. (address in *Poet's Market* or *Songwriter's Market*), and pay that official body to copyright each poem and keep a record of it on hand. A rather expensive proposition, but only you know how badly you need to copyright (with a seemingly ironclad padlock) any of your work. Some take the much cheaper route, mailing pieces back to themselves and just not opening the envelope, collecting future, officially-stamped proof of their authorship, and the *latest possible time* of authorship. In all honesty, however, I'd rather hold on to those Postal Service contributions, and buy some tasty Mal-o-Mars.

When you get to the "book" phase (yes, even a POETRY collection), you will put *Copyright 20__, Al Rocheleau (or whoever), All Rights Reserved* on it. You can send away for that U. S. Copyright Office certification now (OK, *somebody* out there's glad that I've "come to my senses"), mailing samples to Washington, D.C. along with a nice check. You'll also want an International Standard Book Number if you're self-publishing (or, another publisher provides it), maybe an ISBN / price bar code, perhaps a Library of Congress Catalog Card Number, and all other manner of goodies— none of which really have to do with the "divine right" of copyrighting— jamming one's staff in one's rock pile and saying, "MINE, ALL MINE! DO NOT TREAD HERE." Anyway, more on the mechanics of publishing will follow.

For now, GET OVER this "serious" fixation on copyrights for your poems, and get back to work, will you. Following the proposition posed by Eliot, they can't steal any great work you haven't gotten around to writing.

IDEAS, IDEAS (THEY'RE EVERYWHERE)

The poet is always on the hunt for fresh perspectives and for new ideas. It can seem that everything that ever was or possibly could be has already been written about, and that every time we scratch a pen on paper or sit at the computer, we risk repeating something, or some-one, if only ourselves. Yet you do continue to write, don't you— and after all these decades, so do I. Somehow or other, even if it is just a different shade or subtle take on a universal theme, we always find our new ideas, new views, and even new audiences to appreciate them.

While I can understand prose writers getting "writer's block," since they must develop salable stories and / or elaborate novel plots, any poet who isn't writing regularly just isn't trying very hard. It's true that confessional poets may dwell on one aspect of their lives, and feel that once they have written a few poems, "baring their soul," that all they can do is engineer variants on that one theme. After a while, perhaps anyone would give up. Well, even strictly confessional poets can use metaphor to analyze themselves and their intimates in subtle fragments, taking indirect routes rather than directly exposing (and venting on, again and again and again) the whole of major incidents in their past. Truth is, it's often those fragments, those casual looks at little things that are most interesting to readers anyway, and easiest to fit into the panorama of their own lives.

But beyond confessionals, let's take a very practical look at what there is to write about. How about... ANYTHING, EVERYTHING. If you'd like some major categories I borrow from all the time, here they are:

ARTS: writing, painting, music, dance, architecture, theater and film— along with takes on specific works of art.

SCIENCE: botany, zoology, physics, geology, anthropology, paleontology, astronomy.

HISTORY: wars, battles, inventions, disasters, acts of heroism, biographies.

GEOGRAPHY: the lands, waters, economies and populations of the world, or a city block.

MYTHOLOGY AND RELIGION: Greek, Roman, Norse, Far Eastern, Native American, Muslim, or Judeo-Christian. The Bible, for instance, has been inspiring poets for centuries. I own real estate there.

OCCUPATIONS AND PASTIMES: the casual doingness of life, of lives; from skyscraper welding to baling hay, from knitting to figure skating; from dialing a rotary telephone, to watching a cockroach pray for his reprieve.

Over the years I have visited and revisited all of these topic (and most sub-topic) areas. All you need to do is take an encyclopedia and go combing. Pick an article (you could almost entertain this as a *random* process) and work with it. Remember, you need not make a major statement; sift out some little detail, explore it, see where it leads. Who knows— whether your future poem is lyric, dramatic, or narrative, and regardless of the form or verse style you choose, right here may contain a seed that you can water, and watch grow in cut glass.

And also, it's possible— the process could even lead you back to a *confessional* poem— albeit one strained through a prism, lightly.

One tack I've tried that works remarkably well in conjuring poems, is to *open a good dictionary.* No, not to find big words to "beef up," or *ruin* a poem— instead, the purpose is to luxuriate, to let word-sounds play on the ear. If certain words play well, and are not so obscure as to be incomprehensible, they might just ring out long enough to spin a good poem around them. Anything that interests you will do. You'll find if you write *interested,* what the reader will read in the end will be *interesting.* Just start somewhere, anywhere even *remotely* intriguing to you, and see how you progress.

Here are two examples, as I recall, from the same page of a dictionary, which included words beginning with the letter "A" as **aa** and **ab.**

SOMETHING ABOUT ARYANS AND JEWS

Aren't we marvelous.

Fine cars, trappings gilded, hair in place
with a breath of flowers
and bold belief in our own superior race.

We ascend the ramp, traverse the arch—
into the abattoir, stupid before stunning
we, the footnotes of history, cry
at once, at length,
our feet stuck,
our motors running.

JESUS OF THE VELDT

The aardwolf pulls and tears
at his carrion in haste
taking the sins of the world
to his shaggy belly.

His shadow eliminates
every hurt and waste—
dissolving to a dusk of landlord
predators, freely.

What were those words whose sounds and images appealed to me? Yes, you probably picked them out with that little hint— ***abattoir*** and ***aardwolf.*** Hopefully, they don't stand out too much. Just enough to help drive a little poem where it's going.

Now, I wrote two poems there in just a few minutes, savoring (and starting from) a few not-so-fancy but interesting words in a diction- ary, just by perusing for pleasure. At home, you no doubt have both an encyclopedia of some kind (covering all the subjects listed), and a dictionary. So, no more attempts at *having* writer's block, OK? Let's move onward in our quest for good ideas.

ON OBSERVATION AND TAKING NOTES: Remember that in pursuit of ideas, small things grow significant almost instantaneously. Then, immediate or eventual, their time comes to debut in an original poem. We don't live in a void, in the black silence of contemplation; rather, we're immersed in images and sounds. Relentless, that stream turns a turbine of senses day and night, the available wattage unused. Our press of hours *seems* routine; then, attuning to the divine power of **observation,** we learn that actually, things are always unique; they are always changing. To *observe* it all, one has to *effect* observation, *know* that one is observing, and *intend* to observe. From this practice will come stark, original snapshots of your surroundings, flashes of lucidity, an appreciating of that *very real apple* pulled in relief from a still-life, snippets of overheard dialogue coming suddenly profound, or some quirk revealed in a no-longer-predictable scene. And *now* that you have observed that way, YOU MUST RECORD.

It's hackneyed, the image of the poet jotting in a notepad, in a journal, or across the faces of napkins inside a corner café. *Let it be.* That one useful cliché I'll allow you— our chapter on *avoiding clichés* notwithstanding. Make it an inviolable *operating procedure:* WRITE DOWN whatever you especially sense or experience, whenever and wherever it occurs. It may be a scene, a fine object suddenly framed, something someone just did, or said, an inflected phrase and then, or later, some twist of words floating to the window of that child's MAGIC 8-BALL that is your mind, forming the line from a future poem that only you could write. Please, don't betray the minor epiphanies of your ears and eyes. All these fragments— WRITE THEM DOWN.

My wife has become used to me bolting out of bed, grasping for a notepad, or the blank back of a gasoline receipt in my wallet, or dashing upstairs to the computer, to get that *one line* down before I forget it. Now, I may not use the line right away. If I'm lucky, I give it a good *title,* a provocative name that will later intrigue me, or I simply save it into a "notebook" e-file. Just as often, the fragment ends up a scribble in a drawer, or in my wallet. Oh no! What about that one, GREAT line?

It's around. What's vital is: I *did* capture it, it's mine, and it will make me smile when I finally use it, since in the end— it *wasn't lost.* As being a poet tends toward lifetime pursuit, we will sift our files, and enjoy like spices for recipes of new poems, the observations, premises, and *lines* we've come to absorb. That is, *if* we wrote them down.

ON DREAMS: There's no question that dreams are a tremendous resource of creative material for the poet. I have had deep, *self-describing* dreams that became poems almost identical to the dreams themselves, with the awakened me seeming only to transcribe. It's true that dreams don't always "make sense," don't always follow a sequential narrative pattern, and may be incomplete in terms resolution of whatever ideas or issues arose like scary or hopeful ether.

Yet dreams, complete or fragmented, present themselves as a factory of aesthetics, with scenes and personages intensely driven, filled with perceived sensations that can, after all, carry their own *innate* sense— almost a kind of super-sense (what I mentioned in the "Poetry as Music" chapter) that cuts across the lines of our waking "reality." The fact is, we can ask how *awake* we are with our eyes open, with the humdrum drumming, and how people within our living scape aren't awake at all until we rouse them with unsuspected doses of art. Our solution: *rescue the ephemeral*— a fragment, a section, the whole dream. Write it down, *right away,* before you forget part, or all of it.

Remember those human voices, the ones that wake us to our *very best* ideas. Each idea, *each one,* is temporal; bereft of plan and action, we may call out, only to watch it drift, and drown.

EDITING, THEN BREATHING

The most grave (and prevalent) mistake among poets, outside of just not writing, is neglect or refusal to *edit*, and *edit again*. Since poems are created with an economy of words, each must be right, or the cumulative effect of "just missing" will be exponential, and can destroy a poem quickly. Since inspiration is a really a quantifiable *luxury*, the best maxim a poet can probably follow is "Forget the Muse— just write something, then edit it!"

Like a sculptor, every small piece of your creation, whether committed to or omitted as the case may be, either adds to or detracts from the whole. The issues to watch for as you edit are:

1. Bad word choices (not quite what you wanted, but some word you "settled for").
2. Clichés, archaic words, quaint word usages or currently "trendy" words.
3. Entire lines or stanzas that say little, or repeat what you've already said.
4. Use of abstract concept words such as "love," "faith," "hope," "fear." SHOW these things; don't just say them.
5. Use of longer words than are necessary, and that gum up the flow (especially use of too many multi-syllabic Latinate words).
6. Obvious ("moon" and "June") rhymes or bad rhymes.
7. Use of multi-syllable rhymes when an extra-sweet or ironic effect is not intended.
8. Extra connecting words (conjunctions, prepositions, articles that aren't really necessary, etc.) used to a) complete

a metered line b) set up an end-rhyme or c) narrate like a prose story.

9.   Incomplete statements, neither supporting nor supported by clear subject nouns, action verbs, and strong object nouns, in main and subordinate clauses.

10. Stand-alone participles or participial phrases that don't tie directly back to the subject of a main or subordinate clause, or pretend, as fragments, to replace simple action verbs.

11. Too many cluttering adjectives and adverbs.

12. Words that stall the flow of the poem, because of sound or number of syllables.

13. Unplanned shifts in viewpoint. (Swapping pronouns.)

14. Unplanned shifts in tense.

15. Use of the passive voice instead of the active voice.

16. Lines that are too long in free verse. (Need to break each line as soon as it feels right.)

17. Uneven meter (too many or too few beats) in fixed forms.

18. Each statement ends on the same line. There's no enjambment, or carrying on to next line.

19. Too much use of direct statement— not enough use of metaphor and simile.

20. Bad metaphors or similes, or ones not reconciled with the actual theme of the poem. Stick to your theme, and constantly refer back to it.

21. Too much alliteration.

22. Incorrect or inconsistent use of punctuation.

23. Incorrect or inconsistent use of capitalized words.

24. Monotonous lack of progression (no beginning, middle, and end.)

25. No special ENDING at all— poem just trails off or stops midstream.

26. A good ending available, but you passed it and so continued the poem too far.

27. Too much actual use of the pronoun "I" in confessional writing (and annoying for the reader who is not you).

28. The presumptuous use of the pronoun "we," encompassing a pronouncement neither original nor profound enough to pretend to take into the fold everyone who reads it.

29. Matter-of-fact narrative, with many unimportant events placed in a sequence; or, narrative all in past tense, without "present-time" dialogue to freshen it.

30. An afterthought of a title, or a title that tells too much about what will follow.

As a matter of fact, you could just turn that *1-thru-30* list into your own **regular checklist**, and run it down on poems you think are "finished." Of course, you may have purposely *allowed* one of items I've noted, or many of them. This is not necessarily wrong— in fact it can be really *right* once in a while. But most of the time you will do (or forget to do) something referred to on that list and as a result, your poem will suffer. Remember that yes, rules were carefully fabricated and polished in order to be broken— but always *intelligently,* and at *calculated* risk. To do that and survive in any manner as an oft-read and appreciated poet, you must first know the rules you're breaking inside and out.

If you're unsure of a word, a line, a stanza, or the entire poem, look at it hard, and ask yourself if you could cite FIVE REASONS why you used that particular thing, or did it that way. Then share your poem with a friend. As in tennis, it's always nice to have a working partner who is currently a bit more proficient than you are— in any case, comments of a good private editor usually beat out "committee" ideas coming from a workshop. Examine closely, however, whatever is said or offered; it may make a difference in the end. Make sure, too, that you've edited the poem as much as you can (if necessary, taking a break from it for a while) before you drop it in another poet's lap. Don't be lazy, because ultimately, your best edits will be *your own.*

Conversely, when you help other poets— and you should, often, because you will learn much about your *own* work while you edit others— be honest, but first consider what's there that is *good*— then go to what you think needs work. Ideally, that poem will have been well edited by its creator before you can view or hear it; therefore, you should find more that's good, or at least interesting, within those lines.

But for God's sake, understand the importance of editing. For a good poet, and anyone who wants to grow in this art and craft, editing comes right before breathing. Working an existing poem to its true point of completion— which could take a minute, an hour, a week or a year— is as important as writing your next poem. You've already come so far, you see— but see also, you're not DONE yet. You must edit thoroughly, *completely,* and then of course, you *do* write the next poem. And edit that one, too.

WORKSHOPS

There are many ways to look at participation in poetry workshops, and as many types of workshops, professional or amateur, to work within. Now, lots of poets abhor the workshop premise and its process, and wouldn't be caught dead in or near one. Others not only swear allegiance to the workshop— they also thrive in that setting. Still some, who *never leave one,* hit a wall and develop no further, partly because of a particular workshop approach. All right; let's break this down.

It is hard to develop as a poet in a complete vacuum. We are, most of us, decidedly *not* Emily Dickinson. A poet needs an audience, whether an audience of one, of twenty, or of thousands. Poetry is, after all, a high form of communication, and an entity that involves, like a battery, two connecting terminals to spark a communication, and ultimately, many points of exchange. Some of those will be simply readers, or listeners, yet hopefully, lovers of poetic utterance. They may not be writers themselves, and even as writers, they may not be specialists in the art of writing poetry.

But in workshops, your audience will be— POETS— new and old, good and bad. And you will be part of that audience, too. Instead of your maintaining a low profile as passive listener or casual reader, the workshop urges you to display your work and have it felt, understood, and critiqued by others.These poets may not operate on the same level of craft that you do, write in the same style, or critique in the same way. They offer feelings that arise while listening to or reading your poem, ideas or conclusions that are provoked— or specifically, *any* items, positive or negative, objective or subjective, that come to them from the poem and its lines.

Here's how a workshop discussion might go. Your participants are Evan, a middle school student who had never previously written a poem; Maryann, a college English major who has been writing poetry since she was a little girl; Blue, the hard-edged poetry-slam guy; Margaret, a cheery housewife just embarking as a serious poet, and Pete, an old salt who has written verse off and on for years. And me, I'll moderate this snippet, like the Stage Manager in *Our Town*.

Evan: I had to write a poem for my class, using a list of words the teacher gave us. Here's the poem. Those words are underlined. I'm not really a poet, though.

LONELY

When you told me, I knew what it was like
to <u>receive</u> a message that a <u>friend</u> had died.

You have been gone a <u>hundred</u> days.

On an <u>acre</u> of tears I <u>built</u> a <u>museum</u> of memories.
The museum is closed; a <u>guard</u> stands
under one <u>fluorescent</u> light. I am the guard.

But whenever you return
it is like something I <u>heard</u> on the <u>radio</u>
about someone <u>lost</u> coming home.

<u>Unbelievable</u> they said.

It is how I feel.

And the museum opens its doors.

Out I <u>tumble</u> into your arms.

Margaret: That's so touching, I feel like crying. Did you lose your mother?

Evan: No, she's in Baltimore. She trained in Dallas to be a flight attendant. Now she has to live in Baltimore for a while, until she can get transferred home. I had to get used to it.

Pete: I got that, kid.

Blue: Yeah— but sticking those pre-fab words into some kind of puzzle ain't poetry, man. I know the teacher made you do it, but it ain't really poetry— it's not organic! It's gotta come from your gut. You need to HOWL out the sadness— that's poetry, man.

Pete: Hey now, leave the kid alone. I know that feeling. It's a quiet feeling, kind of empty, and these are quiet lines.

Moderator: But what about the use of "tumble" at then end? How quiet is a tumble?

Maryann: THAT's where the sadness really comes out, where it gets released. I like the use of that word there.

Moderator:	Poems are all about tension and release.
Margaret:	I loved the "museum of memories"— that's true— memories are kept in your mind like a museum keeps paintings, or maybe, all the artifacts of your life. That's a good metaphor.
Blue:	What's an acre of tears? How do you get an acre of tears? Acres are more about land, right? Tears are water. Don't like that one.
Moderator:	Hey Blue, what DO you like? Find something.
Maryann:	Evan, how did you decide where to put spaces between lines?
Evan:	I have no idea. I guess because the thoughts came to me one at a time.
Margaret:	Perhaps some of the lines can be shortened, so they don't read like a story.
Pete:	Well, poems can tell a story. But yeah, maybe some of the lines could be shortened.
Margaret:	And I think you needed to put quotation marks around "Unbelievable" because it's a quote.
Maryann:	It is a quote, but—

Blue:	So it's a quote. Doesn't matter. He's not writing in the newspaper. It's a poem. He calls the shot. It's OK to leave it like that. There, that's something I like. No marks.
Pete:	I like that you are the guard in the poem, Evan. You talk about a guard, and then you say YOU are the guard. That surprised me. How you guard the museum.
Blue:	Maybe I would tear that museum down man. Right in the poem. Tell your mom to come home for good.
Moderator:	That's a different point of view, Blue— that could be another poem, a different one.
Blue:	Yeah, I think I'll write *that* one, man.
Pete:	Good work, Evan.
Evan:	Thanks. I like what you said about making some lines shorter. I think that would be good to do.
Moderator:	Actually, this was a great job Evan— especially having to work with all those words you were given.
Maryann:	Yes Evan, it WAS great job!

Anyway, that's more or less the rundown. Sometimes— not often, thankfully— workshops can turn into a free-for-all among those who think they know everything— and don't. They will pick and pick, thinking criticism has to be what's *wrong*, not what's *right*, and *why*. (After years of conducting workshops or participating in them, I've occasionally pondered how to otherwise spend my time— maybe bowling— or writing a one-act satire that presents the quirkiest and most irritating characters and aspects of the "poet game," called... *Lucifer's Workshop.* If only Buñuel were alive to film it!) But in fact, a badly-run workshop and its uncorrected chemistry will at long last fail, as the loudest or "most experienced" voice instills an intimidat-ing *group-think* that is harmful to everyone— *especially* to a new poet who needs encouragement to continue.

Of course, an opposite scenario also robs our profit. Workshops can empty themselves of any true analysis to the point that they become little galas of "I'm so good, and you are, too." Neither of the barren frontiers we've marked should be a destination. When your moderator is a good one (and sometimes a very good poet, too) he will keep the philistines in line, and endeavor to bring out something in each writer, making them observe and consider, not only when that poet's own work is under critique, but also when the *same* poet is *critiquing.* The moderator knows that in the end, the "critic" may learn more about *his own work* by *constructively* examining someone else's. Repeating the **Rule of Thumb,** or if you like, **Thumb Up**— start a critique of some-one's poem with what *worked* for you, then go to what didn't.

In various parts of the country, celebrated poets, sometimes alone or sometimes in tandem, conduct professional workshops. Attendance at these could be open to a hundred registrants, or limited to just a few.

A typical agenda can include lectures, readings, and personal or group critiques. Some events are quite technical in nature, and some are so freewheeling as to never mention forms, sound devices, meter, etc.

A colleague of mine attended a small workshop conducted by Sharon Olds some years ago. Ms. Olds's apt student, now well published, told me the event could have been conducted at the Cassadaga Spiritualist Camp between seances, or during the big rainstorm at the Woodstock Festival— *yet she loved it!* However free-form such workshops may be philosophically, they can be *exactly* what some poets need to open up their perspective on their art. (Anne Sexton was notorious for her Isadora Duncan-like approach to college seminars; unpredictable and darkly funny, the muse of Newton could certainly fill a room.)

Ultimately, the purpose of workshops, whether online or in person, and conducted on whatever amateur or professional level— is to share, to encourage, and to gain or impart knowledge, ideas, inspiration. If you're getting none of those at the workshop you now attend, drop it. Attending NO workshop is better for a developing poet than suffering through a bad one. But if you do need (or want to provide) any of those special commodities within your locale, seek a out a *good* workshop, or maybe even *start one.*

And by the way, Evan's mom did get home soon enough; unlike all of us, Evan never felt the need to write another poem, though he did write *that* one. Evan is my son.

POETRY LIVE, YOU AND OTHERS

For many years, I eschewed a local poetry scene in favor of my tasks in the virtual one, working and commiserating with poets online in the U.S. and around the world. But eventually I decided my reverse parochialism was wrongheaded, so I ventured out into the evening breeze and was glad I did. While the poetry community in many actual, not virtual, places may be small, quirky, and even strangely political, every poet owes it to themselves and others to get involved there on some level.

Through local workshops and readings, poets can often learn and grow. By taking part, these poets may contribute to others by way of input and support, and in turn, be helped and supported. It's true that you should pick your shots; as we've said, some workshops are not well organized, and could be lorded over by self-involved idiots.

Likewise, regular readings may be stacked in favor of certain poets or certain styles of poetry, and you may not feel comfortable in that particular "circle of friends." Undaunted, shake the dust from your footwear and move down the road or, in a big city, across the street. Just as there are lots of poets out there, there are lots of poetry groups.

If you can't find one, and don't know a lot of local poets, use the internet and the profiles of its various social networking sites to find some. Communicate with those poets, share work, and if their demeanor, level of development, etc., is compatible, who knows, you may be on your way to starting your own little group, getting together at coffee shops or homes to critique work, or to stage readings.

TYPES OF READINGS

Some events will involve featured readers; these are poets already known to the organizers and possibly to the local poetry community, invited to participate, and possibly promoted. There can be one or more of these readers, and they will read several or many poems in an allotted time span. When that part of the program is completed, an "open-microphone" session will usually fill the time remaining.

During "open mike," any poet can get up to read, usually *one* poem. Note that there may not be much time remaining in the event. If a poet intends to read, he or she should have their selected poem in hand, and be ready to come forward when there is an obvious opening or when summoned by the organizer.

Customarily at the start of the evening, poets who wish to read will sign up on a sheet of paper and will read, time permitting, by order in which they signed. But a reading list is not used at all readings, and in that case, poets raise their hand to be called on by the organizer, or just walk to the podium (or mike) when it is free.

More often, readings are entirely "open mike"— meaning there's usually plenty of time for anyone who wants to read. Based on the number of probable readers however, the number of poems a poet reads is still usually held to one or two. (Obviously, a very long poem is not a good one to pull out at a group reading, unless of course, you are the *featured reader,* and so have an ample amount of time given to you.) The reading sign-up list, organizer call-ups, or open podium etiquette apply here as in the previous set-up. The extra time that is available for open-mike readers to read (or if they are new, to muster a bit of courage first) is the only difference.

POETRY SLAMS

Poetry slams have proliferated in the past decade; in fact, ceremonial versions of these "rites" were common in ancient cultures, those that revered their poets as priests. *Slams* are poetry reading competitions. The original work of two or more (and often many) poets are pitted against one another and graded by the crowd or selected judges. Poets can be graded by ballot and scored for poem content *and* delivery— tantamount to a figure skating or gymnastics contest— or simply made subject to the volume of applause. Slams lend themselves to energetic "performance" styles, and many poems are hard-edged and highly rhythmic so as to involve the crowd. Performance poetry may contain dramatic oratory, comedy, role-playing, movement around the stage, and even props. Usually, there is more than one round, possibly with elimination rounds, so poets prepare more than one poem. The poets read with or without microphone, and usually without podium. Poems are delivered with flourish from sheets of paper, performed from memory, or even improvised. Crowds are supportive; the degree of support, however, isn't uniform. If you take part, know that:

1. Your poem(s) may not be of a style that wholly fits the mood of the crowd.

2. You may not have the performance qualities the crowd is looking for (generally, the more flamboyant or unique, the better).

3. They may like your poem, but simply like someone else's better, and score you accordingly on their relative scale.

Therefore, you do need thicker skin to take part here. It's entertaining to engage other poets at slams (I have done so), but it's just as much fun to watch. The quality of the poems heard is quite uneven, since performance often counts for more than does the actual lyric content. (For me, that's when I don't mind losing.) At some point, I bet you'll want to try this, and you should. Just pick poems that are on the hard-edged or comedic side of your art, let that inner actor come out, and *just wing it!*

MORE ABOUT READINGS— NOT TO WORRY

If you go to a reading, any reading, you don't need to read. You will likely enjoy yourself anyway, meet other poets, and by your presence alone lend support to those poets who do read, as well as to the poetry community itself. So go. But when you do, at least consider actually *reading.* Yes, you. Perhaps the first time, or anytime you don't have material of your own to hand, you can bring up a poem written by someone else, perhaps a master poet you like. These are always just as well received as original work, and may not be as challenging for a new reader to deliver. That said, let's not dissuade you from taking your own work up *the very first time you go,* and introducing yourself via your own poems to the community.

You'll note that poets who read are not all great. Many are not great *at all,* at least not yet, but they have worked to the degree they have worked, and they are not wrong to want to be heard. Ultimately, to be heard and read is why we write; that sentiment must include you. Now, you *should* develop a lot of material, and you *must* polish it. There comes a time, however, when it's OK to share your poem, to read it with all the mood or passion that had informed you to write it. Sure, you may be nervous, and you'll see others nervous at times. It's all right; it's almost expected. Go up there and read. Don't worry, the folks will be supportive— they always are.

FORMULA FOR A FIRST READING (BUT PROBABLY <u>NOT</u> A SLAM)

1. Write good poems as well as you can write them.

2. Edit them and edit them. Reading aloud can help.

3. *Practice* reading your best, finished poems. This is where you perfect your delivery.

4. Read slowly, directly; don't look down. Do project outward, and don't slur your words. It's good to vary your dynamics a bit, working to find the cadences and music in that poem. A "groove" exists in which a piece will positively ride; you'll find it, if you practice. Know that your voice is *your own,* unique; your delivery and cadence, yours, too. One trendy gimmick— and contrary to our aims— is what I call "National Public Radio (NPR) reading." In this elite act of lethargy (insidious in ways that could someday take a *small* public audience for poetry and make it *extinct* as a gaggle of Great Auks), poets too knowingly "profound" for their own good speak in patronizing faux-tones and blah cadences, with every line-end turned up sweetly like they are telling stories to three-year-olds! Forget it; just be *you.*

5. OK. Find a reading out there and go to it.

6. Perhaps you go a time a two and don't read at first, but you go, listen, learn.

7.   When you go and you *want* to read, get yourself on the "reading list."

8.   Select your poem from a group of several. You're bound to find one that fits your mood or the group's mood best at that point. Maybe none of the poems you brought seem to fit. Well, take a chance on one anyway.

9.   Have the selected poem to hand (I usually print out the poems in a large font size, so I can read them easily), and sip water or a Coke before rising to assure that the lips, mouth, and throat are moist.

10.   Sometimes, readings don't have lists, and if not, raise your hand to be called up by the organizer; if this is not happening, wait for an opening and just walk up on your own.

11.   If there's a microphone / podium set-up, make sure the mike is at the right level to pick up your voice. You may want to introduce yourself, but if the precedent has not been set, don't concern yourself. Me, I just say, "Hi, I'm Al, and this poem is called such-and-such." You might take a casual breath in, and slowly blow it out. Then take another, relax, and deliver the poem.

12.   Remember, make it direct, slow enough, loud enough; avoid burying your face in the poem. Look up periodically at one sympathetic face, then at another (there *will* be some, I promise!), or look slightly over the crowd.

13. Don't speed up as you go in order to "get it over with." That defeats the courage you have already shown. Read on; and stay in that "groove."

14. Most of the time there will be applause, but not always at all readings; take that in stride. And should some applaud, enjoy it! Either way, you accomplished your goal.

15. Support in kind others who read, showing them your your appreciation, and become a regular at such events.

There you have it.

Each time you read, it gets easier, and you become better known. So does your work, and this inspires you to write more, edit more, read more, etc. Hooked once, this may all become a regular habit— a good one. Ask the local veterans of this communal process; they'll tell you the same.

And welcome to the community, poet.

JUNKIES (OPEN POETRY READING, 7 PM)

So here again—
without a stall, or stadium.

I recognize faces,
cubist angles, countenances from Dante
or the back corner

of Birdland,
smacked up in the cold light.

We have a point.
What silvers the vein,
aesthetic hum of an anesthetic presence
desires an audience,
an ear, a commiseration.

We understand the strap in the teeth,
the lines along a dull tattoo,
the dizzy, shameless
deliberate self.

Once I told an acquaintance
who thought to dabble
that commitment falls like cement off a ruin,
buries you but, done right
(shiny, white)
is each time a final, fertile slice
of sex and deliverance.

Which brings us here—

to a mass if not a cure,
the string within a shibboleth
pulled at, something cheap,
eviscerating,
paramount and pure.

PUBLISHING YOUR WORK: PART ONE

Seems we got to the end of this little book so quickly. (Well, maybe you knew what you were doing already, and just *started* with this chapter.) The flow of instruction, such as it appears, was designed for steady distribution to poets over a period of a year; we now have only this chapter and two more, related ones left. After that, I expect that some may, to quote Gertrude Stein, "actively repeat it all"— yes, right from the beginning. Should any person want to become "versed" in a study, it's good to read the material more than once. Throughout this book, we've covered every major aspect of writing poetry— all for what comes now— *getting published.* If you've applied all that came before, this part should be easy.

Here's a pronouncement that will perhaps surprise you. **GOOD WORK WILL GET PUBLISHED.** Outside of picking wrong or really difficult markets, the only reason poets DON'T get published is: *they are sending out substandard work.* I have heard every other excuse there is, *twice;* ultimately, it's only the above that counts for a serious poet who INTENDS to publish. There is a huge market out there for your work. And anyone who offers the usual "I only write for myself," or " I can't get published because it's all political," or "I just don't have time to submit," is *grrrrrr,* just so full of— Jonathan Swift employs the word as a verb in "The Lady's Dressing Room"— but for *nouns,* check that "origin-of-words list" on Page 52. Actually, the only other "obstacle," good poems available, is: **you want to get work published, but you don't know how.** THAT ONE we can work with, because yes, it's true, politics be damned, all it really takes for a poet to succeed is: **good, edited, finished work,** and what follows.

GETTING YOUR POEMS READ AND IN PRINT:

While workshops and readings bring the poet in touch with the world of his peers, creating camaraderie, mutual support, and quite possibly, local recognition— in the end, all you may do as a working poet leads to *this*— you HAVE to get work *in print*. If not, well, it's like reading about sex or mountain climbing without ever having tried them. *It's just not quite the same thing.* Forget the contests; forget vanity presses and paid "anthologies." You must publish in **quality** magazines and journals that **a)** accept work only on the work's own merit, and without fee; **b)** display good work among other poets' work of same or better merit; **c)** have some actual circulation and readership; and **d)** have an appearance that care was taken, regardless of limited budget (and many are limited) to display the work in a professional manner. Even considering all those points, you'd be surprised how large a field there is for good poems, and just how GREAT you'll feel as you begin to be published. Without question, it will change forever your outlook on your work, and on your own future as a "working" poet.

With all that in mind, we invite you to consider the following.

PRINT IS PERMANENCE, AND A VALIDATION OF HARD WORK: There are over 2,000 small magazines in this country. The way to pursue publication, once you have a finished body of poems (say, a dozen, or two dozen very good ones), is to package three, four, or five poems per packet, and send them to journals you've scouted out in *Poet's Market. Poet's Market* is a bible of sorts for working poets. It tells you to whom, what, where, when, why, and how to submit your poems to those most likely to publish exactly what you have. All the submission information for each market is there, including a rating system for types of markets, as well as their expectations. This

important tool costs about $25.00, and a new, updated version comes out every year, usually by September. Use it.

Decide the *relative worth* of each of your poems (is this poem a major statement, are those minor ones, and where would they fit best given the subject or style), and target your locations for submission on the basis of, get this— *how many times you expect to be rejected.* Yes, you need to be hard-boiled. Poetry publishing is for tough people.

Now, if you pick the top magazines (noted in *Poet's Market* before each listing by a circular icon that is **three-quarters full,** meaning they prefer poems from highly-skilled, experienced poets)— even if it's *excellent* work, you could be rejected 15-20 times— in truth, were talking Vegas odds here. (The finest journals may get *tens of thousands* of submissions each year.) If you choose the next level down (an icon with a circle that is **half full,** meaning they prefer submissions from skilled, experienced poets, but will consider submissions from beginners)— again, even if it's first-rate work, it stands to be rejected perhaps 8-10 times. Be prepared.

It's fine to start with the *lowest-level* markets (represented by an icon with a **completely open circle,** meaning they readily accept worthy poems from beginners— really, some of these markets are still *very* good). Based on the scope of your poems, and on your confidence— select your market level, knowing you can always re-send poems to a lower-level publication if the poems seem to be continually bombing out on the level above. Yet even on the "beginners readily accepted" level, good work could be rejected anywhere from 1-5 times, depending on the type of publication and the needs and wants of the editor. You must get used to that; it's part of the game.

One important tip-off for possible acceptance is the percentage of submissions a magazine publishes. If it's *less than 5% per year,* the odds for each submission will not be great; but if you believe in the poems and in that publication, you take your chances.

Include a cover letter— unless an editor's listing specifically tells you he doesn't need one. (Note that electronic submissions are now becoming more prevalent and convenient for everyone; these may not require information beyond the poems themselves.) If you are unsure, always use the cover letter. In the letter, tell the editor a *few* defining items about yourself, where you've been published, if you have yet, and if you haven't, *that* you haven't but why you selected the editor's magazine to try to break in. (An example follows in the final chapter.) You'd be surprised at what may come of that simple cover letter— it could make a difference, all other things (and poems) being equal.

Before I forget, you include with your submission **a self-addressed, stamped envelope (SASE)** for the return of any poems that are not accepted. (Sometimes a magazine will request loose stamps for the return, so that usable stamps are not wasted. Let's face it, postal costs are ever rising for everyone.) Use of the SASE is standard for mailed submissions, unless otherwise instructed in the market listing.

ON THE RISE OF "E-MAGAZINES (E-ZINES)":
Note also that internet-based "e-magazines" or "e-zines" have created a market all their own. In past decades, many poets, including me, looked down on these efforts because of their *(at the time)* primitive construction, the quality of the poetry represented, and the impermanent lifespans of publications compared to print magazines, the latter of which, even decades later, can still *physically* exist.

With time and more technology, maturity has come to the electronic marketplace— and there are many e-magazines that exude quality in their layouts, navigation facility, audio capacity, and excellence of the poets and poems represented. Some, such as *Rose and Thorn Journal, Cortland Review, DMQ (Disquieting Muses Quarterly),* and *Melic Review* have won numerous awards, and are now considered among the top poetry magazines in the United States, regardless of media type. Similar magazine sites are now flourishing in the U.K., Canada, France, Australia and other countries around the world.

While you must still separate wheat from chaff, e-magazines will add to your list of markets. While most of us will always have affinity for print magazines that we can hold in our own hands and savor, these e-zines now have their own "pull" and staying power. Even if a site may someday cease operation, your poems are secured in places where they may be accessed indefinitely via today's excellent search engines, obviating to some extent the "permanency" concern. (As a bonus, the cycle of *electronic submissions and replies* tends to be much faster.)

The reality is, good magazines are good magazines whenever and wherever you find them. Ultimately, you know their worth by the unmistakable quality they offer. Of course, those good magazines make for good markets, and then, upon your success in submitting to them, they fashion the "credits list" for your career. So enjoy the hunt.

Now, let's go deeper into the process of submissions, and move on to the end of your apprenticeship or simple brush-up as a working poet.

PUBLISHING YOUR WORK: PART TWO— BUILDING THE MACHINE

We've stated flat-out that publishing is hard work. But like all work, it's easier to accomplish when you get a machine to help you out. What has been successful for this writer, with 100-or-so poems published in journals in the past decade, and for many other poets who know the same routine, is: you must build a *submission machine.*

As a hedge against rejections, you must get out as many good (and non-duplicated) packets of poetry as you can at the same time. When a packet returns, and there aren't any acceptances in the bunch, send the poems to your next candidate. IMMEDIATELY. Don't stew over a rejection. If they accepted one or more poems in the packet, great; now take the ones that didn't get accepted and work them into a new packet ready to go out. List possible new markets for each packet (and their poem types) ahead of time. RUN IT LIKE A REAL MACHINE, but don't submit the same work simultaneously to more than one magazine. *You wait for the response—* that's part of the process. Good material WILL get accepted, and in journals that you choose— not in amateur "contests" or ersatz "anthologies"— rather, we're talking real month-in / month-out publishing— *imagine that.*

NOTE: There *are* some very good contests sponsored by excellent magazines and organizations, and to these you might want to enter poems, or even a collection of poems. Such contests are listed in their own section of *Poet's Market.* Sometimes an entity does require a small entry fee which is divided between future prize money and support of the magazine or organization itself. The larger magazines and organizations are better funded, and those don't usually charge fees.

Anyway, response time from a publisher on your packet could range from as little as 2 weeks, to 4 or 5 *months.* Many magazines publish infrequently (*note* what months they accept material)— so you wait. Pass the time by reading, writing, editing, submitting other material, and re-submitting. Again, do not simultaneously submit material to more than one mag, unless each one of them states that they accept **simultaneous submissions.** As a rule, *just don't simultaneously submit at all.* Have enough work out there that the wait doesn't worry you, and know that the waiting itself is part of becoming a professional at what you do. Be professional.

By all means, KEEP TRACK of where your work is. A real momentum-breaker is loose organization, where you forget (and you WILL) where you sent exactly what. Start a notebook (or a computer file) that lists what the submissions were, where you sent them, and when you sent them. This way, you'll ensure you never send the same poem to the same mag, though you may yet want to send others to them, if you really like that mag. (One rejection doesn't mean they'll ALL be rejected there!) Also, the aforementioned file will let you know when a magazine needs to be "nudged" about giving you an answer on your work. If the time has gone beyond what they tell you is their consideration period, you have a right to ask, courteously, by letter or e-mail, whether your work has been considered yet, and whether you should wait a bit longer or submit the poems elsewhere.

Now, how do you get, say, 20-30 accepted poems per year? In good markets? Well, work you submit *must* be good, finished material— well-edited by you, not slapped together in a night or at a weekend workshop. Packets should contain 3 to 5 poems (and be sure that the line-counts fit the mag's requirements). The strength of the respective packets must reflect the strength of the markets at which you're aiming. A lower-level market might dictate you using one of your best poems as an anchor, combined with a few that while good, aren't quite AS accomplished, or at least as ambitious. A major market, however, will require three to five of your *very best* in order to give you any shot at acceptance.

Obviously, the more fine work you have to submit, the more flexible you can be with your submissions— to the point that you just can't wait for a rejection to come back so that you can send out to the *next* good market you had in mind, but had foolishly ranked SECOND for that packet, behind the one that just turned you down! (That's right— you *have* to believe in your work. Think that way.)

Always pick markets that fit your work. Don't send political poems to a love poetry mag, or sonnets to a "Beat" journal that uses only free verse. Don't send a wildly confessional piece to an inspirational / religious magazine, and so on. If you're not sure what a journal's content is really like, it never hurts to send for a sample. Align a particular market (chosen essentially by level of difficulty in your bible, *Poet's Market*) to a particular grouping of poems, based on the scope of the poems, the refinement of craft, and, once more— how many times you are willing to risk rejection.

Remember— *more difficult the market, more chance for rejection.* And also, don't forget the magazine's ratio of acceptances to poems received. Under 5% will mean a tough market, even on a lower-level rating in the book— but it may *still* be the market you have in mind, and if you do— go after it.

Repeat. Very Important. Unless otherwise instructed by a prospective editor, which won't be often— you must produce a good **COVER LETTER** to accompany each packet. In our final chapter, we'll show you a model. What happens: you get rejected a lot at first. Steel yourself; maybe the ratio of acceptances from individual packets you submit will be 1 in 20. Later, as you know your markets better, and learn how to weigh the relative merits of your work (hence, judge the very best destinations for each poem), your ratio could improve to 1 in 10. Eventually, it will get even better than that. Over the years, it did for me, and for thousands of other poets the same. As long as there are thousands of markets, too— and there are— your prospects for successfully placing work in quality publications will always be good. It's just a question of potential— not *existence* of potential— that's already with you, inside you. What we are talking about, confidently, is the *realization* of it.

COVER LETTERS, ETC., AND... YOU'RE ON YOUR WAY!

We begin the final chapter with an example of a cover letter to accompany your packets of poems that you submit to publishers. Here's one to use once you have some past credits to lean on:

> Molly Jones
> 3232 Frost Circle
> Fall River, MA 02720

August 13, 20__

John Smith, Editor
Equus
PO Box 345
Olathe, KS 66051

Dear Mr. Smith,

Enclosed please find three poems I am submitting to *Equus* for your consideration. They are: "Culpa," "Sea Grapes," and "Scott County."

My work has appeared in *Nedge, Haight Ashbury Literary Journal,* and *Mobius.* I selected your publication because of the quality of the writing, and the scope of its content. I would be honored to be represented in *Equus,* and look forward to your response.

Sincerely,

Molly Jones

Simple and to the point, right? Some poets elect to buy copies of the magazine or send away for a sample, and then enclose a line complimenting the magazine by citing more detail about its content or specific poems they liked. But me, I prefer it ultra-simple and straightforward. No self-aggrandizement, no blathering, no buttering up the editor, no sob-story.

Now, if you have no credits yet, try this in the body of the letter:

> "I have been writing for ____ years, but have only recently decided to place what I feel may be some of my best work. I know that you have published the work of new poets, and I felt *Equus* was the right selection for consideration of these poems; I thank you for your time reviewing them. I would be honored to be represented in *Equus,* and look forward to your response."

NOTE: Most markets *don't* accept simultaneous submissions, but some do, and if they do, they state it.

If you are simultaneously submitting a poem (or poems) to other magazines— and only if those magazines have all stated that they accept simultaneous submissions— you should include a sentence affirming your decision to so submit. It's only fair to all of them; in addition, your telling each might speed up the decision-making process, if an editor really likes your poem(s).

And once again— don't forget to include that *self-addressed, stamped envelope* for returns.

ABOUT REJECTIONS

Don't worry about them. Repeat. *Don't worry about them.* I've published many poems in many markets, but I've had five times as many submissions rejected. Believe me, the first acceptance that you receive in a legitimate journal, you'll forget every rejection that came before it. Often, submissions are not rejected on your's work merit; rather, the editor simply has too many poems backlogged to consider more. Also, you may have sent poems that don't fit the editorial slant or need (KNOW YOUR MARKETS!!); or, an editor could have really liked your work, but in ranking poems taken from a large selection, it was a "just missed." All of that happens. And don't get upset at "form" rejections, in which the editor doesn't comment. Those replies occur most of the time. Of course, it's always nice to get a personal note, especially an encouraging one. Just don't expect it.

While I've had my successes in very good markets in the U.S. and abroad, one treasured *rejection* I received carries as much weight with me as do many acceptances. In what was obviously a letter that took the editor some time to write (I had received a few form rejections from this magazine over the years), this gentleman apologized for a long delay in responding, discussed the poem packet I sent, said he enjoyed the work, and that some of the poems came very close to his needs, but... not quite. He invited me to submit again. The editor was **Joseph Parisi,** longtime editor of ***Poetry,*** the best-known poetry journal in the world, the journal that introduced the work of T. S. Eliot, Ezra Pound, Marianne Moore, and Wallace Stevens. So you see, every rejection has value, and some more than others! Just keep writing, and submitting; await the day each excellent poem finds its home. (By the way, those Parisi-poems did acquire their own good placements elsewhere.)

FAREWELL (FOR THIS BOOK, AT LEAST)

In this manual we presented suggestions, guidelines, examples, and...
that's all. In the end, everything you do as a poet is up to you. Let's
face it, the most fun a poet has is "breaking the rules." But to be a
good poet, you can't break the rules WELL until you know some. The
topics we've covered are basic to all poetry, all styles. I hope the
pieces, at least some of them, have helped. You are important enough
for me to have written such a book. It has been an honor for me to do
that for you. If the book helps you or someone you know, now or later,
it was worth writing.

Which leads me to reiterate that final measure that goes into publishing well and often— DON'T EVER GIVE UP. Poetry is a tough pursuit, with little thanks other than your own satisfaction. And the most
satisfaction you'll get is in developing your craft, followed by seeing
your good work in print, and having it appreciated by a universe of
eyes, and ears. Since few of us, as poets, may gain major celebrity or
wealth in the literary world doing what it is we love— any more than
sandlot shortstops may get to turn double plays at Yankee Stadium—
we hone our craft, realize our art, and get our voice heard. If *you* can
do that, *you're a poet,* advancing at last, some small part of a culture
in need. Yes, by vocation, a POET, a real one—not a make-believe
one— and that's something to be proud of. It starts wherever you are
right now, novice or current practitioner, and it goes on from there.
And if you work at it, your art, your craft, you can only progress, only
succeed. So there you are! Pass the champagne— we're finished—
and you've begun.

For though the poet's matter nature be,
His art doth give the fashion; and, that he
Who casts to write a living line, must sweat,
(Such as thine are) and strike the second heat
Upon the Muses' anvil; turn the same
(And himself with it) that he thinks to frame,
Or, for the laurel, he may gain a scorn;
For a good poet's made, as well as born;
And such wert thou. Look how the father's face
Lives in his issue, even so the race
Of Shakespeare's mind and manners brightly shines
In his well-turned, and true-filed lines;
In each of which he seems to shake a lance,
As brandish'd at the eyes of ignorance.

from "To the Memory of My Beloved,
the Author, Mr. William Shakespeare"

— Ben Jonson

ABOUT THE AUTHOR

Al Rocheleau's work has appeared in over 40 magazines and journals in the United States, Canada, the U.K., France, Austria, and Poland. Publications include the *Haight Ashbury Literary Journal, Sahara, Poetry Salzburg Review, Outerbridge, Mockingbird, Poetry Depth Quarterly, Pig Iron,* and *ArtWord Quarterly.* Al has hosted two popular online poetry workshops; from 1998-2002, he was Poetry Editor and Senior Columnist at *Amazing Instant Novelist,* a writer's website sponsored by America Online. Al's instructional pieces have appeared in several magazines, and in resource databases at various colleges, high schools and middle schools. In 2004, he was awarded the Thomas Burnett Swann Poetry Prize by the Gwendolyn Brooks Writers Association of Florida. Al has completed three poetry collections, and is currently compiling a general education manual and syllabus for parents who home-school secondary grade-level students. He lives in Orlando, Florida.

CONTACTING AL ROCHELEAU

Al Rocheleau has dedicated four decades of his life to poetry and to helping poets do and be the best they can. He has always made himself accessible to anyone in need, and that extends beyond this book. For questions, comments, and assistance, you can contact Al through the publisher, Shantih Press, via e-mail, ARRO40@aol.com, or write to: P.O. Box 770640, Orlando, FL 32877-0640.